D0961454

SIMPLIFY

RICHARD KOCH
and
GREG LOCKWOOD

Foreword by Perry Marshall, Author of
80/20 Sales and Marketing

Entrepreneur
PRESS®

Entrepreneur Press, Publisher
Cover Design: Andrew Welyczko
Production and Composition: Ponderosa Pine Design

First published in Great Britain in 2016 by Piatkus, an imprint of the Little, Brown Book Group.
Richard Koch and Greg Lockwood have asserted their right to be identified as authors of this Work.

This publication is designed to provide accurate and authoritative information in regard to the subject matter covered. It is sold with the understanding that the publisher is not engaged in rendering legal, accounting or other professional services. If legal advice or other expert assistance is required, the services of a competent professional person should be sought.

Library of Congress Cataloging-in-Publication Data

Names: Koch, Richard, 1950- author. | Lockwood, Greg, author.
Title: Simplify : how the best businesses in the world succeed / Richard
  Koch, Greg Lockwood ; foreword by Perry Marshall.
Description: First American Edition. | Irvine : Entrepreneur Press, 2016. |
  Originally published: London : Piatkus, 2016.
Identifiers: LCCN 2016029110| ISBN 9781599185996 (hardback) | ISBN
1599185997
Subjects: LCSH: Success in business. | Leadership. | BISAC: BUSINESS &
  ECONOMICS / Small Business. | BUSINESS & ECONOMICS /
Development /
  Business Development. | BUSINESS & ECONOMICS / Leadership. |
BUSINESS &
  ECONOMICS / Advertising & Promotion.
Classification: LCC HF5386 .K7634 2016b | DDC 658.4/012--dc23
LC record available at https://lccn.loc.gov/2016029110

Printed in the United States of America
20 19 18 17 16   10 9 8 7 6 5 4 3 2 1

For Christina and Zoe
– Greg

For Matthew, Jamie, Justin, and Peter
– Richard

Contents

PART TWO: HOW TO SIMPLIFY

PART THREE: SAVE THE DINOSAURS?

PART FOUR: THE REWARDS OF SIMPLIFYING

Foreword

PERRY MARSHALL

This is not just a "great" book. Nor is it merely an important book, or a "good read." SIMPLIFY is one of the ten most valuable business books you will read in your lifetime. I charged $7000 a head for a three day seminar with Richard in Chicago. The event culminated in five hours of Richard delivering his SIMPLIFY material. This audience included entrepreneurs with $10 million+ businesses, with potential to reach into the billions. They were ecstatic.

SIMPLIFY is a shortcut to the exact business that will game-change any industry. Business people and investors talk about "unicorns," "disruptive business models," and all the rest. Those superstars are hard to predict, but we know them when we see them — usually *after* the big money has already been made. This book leaps you past years of meandering to the exact product or service that will tip the playing field solidly in your favor. If you pull this off, your competitors will find it impossible to follow you. And you will make life-changing money.

The real title of this book could very well be, *SIMPLIFY: If you don't, they will.* That's because it is inevitable that sooner or later, someone will come along and revolutionize your industry. It will typically be an outsider — like Larry Page and Sergey Brin upsetting the search engine industry with Google. The good ol' boys club rarely sees the outsiders coming until it's too late.

It *will* happen. The question is, who is going to do it? It can be you. Even if you're insider. If you know the formula.

This is not just a book to read and enjoy. (Though it is a very enjoyable read.) This is a book to memorize, to internalize, whose ideas should permeate your thinking, your planning, and the language you share with your investors and key team members.

Richard worked harder on this book than any other. It was a massive undertaking. Simplification always is.

Oliver Wendell Holmes famously said "For the simplicity that lies this side of complexity, I would not give a fig, but for the simplicity that lies on the other side of complexity, I would give my life." What he means by this is, our initial conceptions of a product or a project are often clear and simple ... then in the middle of the project things get almost hopelessly complex. Most people never get out of the woods.

But on rare occasions, a visionary like Steve Jobs has a clear vision for achieving simplicity and elegance and doggedly pursues this to the end. That vision is what Richard defines in this book. We've heard all the stories about Jobs' obsession with simplicity, but here Richard lays it all out in a succinct formula that mere mortals can achieve. He has embodied simplicity even in his teaching of it.

Richard sent me several drafts and we spent months discussing it. His final product is genius. I don't know if it will outsell his famous book *The 80/20 Principle*; it may not, as this material is highly advanced.

But it doesn't matter. Because *this* is Richard Koch's Magnum Opus.

Preface

RICHARD KOCH

For the past forty years I have searched for simple, elemental, elegant, and parsimonious principles that will help individuals create great new businesses, and thus enrich the world and the people involved.

Principles are wonderful things, because if they are really powerful they can save us enormous effort and stop us going down dead ends. In science and business there are just a few such principles; but whereas most scientists are aware of the beautiful principles in their field, few business people are guided by principles in their daily work, preferring to rely on *methods* — the next level down. Yet, as the nineteenth-century philosopher Ralph Waldo Emerson said, "As to methods there may be a million and then some, but principles are few. The man who grasps principles can successfully select his own methods. The man who tries methods, ignoring principles, is sure to have trouble."

To qualify, a principle must be so overwhelmingly powerful that ordinary mortals — such as you or me — can reliably create extraordinary results, not through personal brilliance, but just by following the principle carefully and with a modicum of common sense.

The principles can tell you which businesses you can create or work within, with a reasonable expectation that if you follow the principles, the business will stand a great chance of success.

Through trial and error, I have had some success in identifying some really stunning principles. If you had asked me four years ago which single principle works best in business, I would have said the *Star Principle*. As you may know, this is my interpretation of the famous "Boston Box," invented by the Boston Consulting Group. Also known as the Growth–Share Matrix, the Boston Box says that every business falls into one of four categories:

- **Star** — the largest business in a high-growth market.
- **Question mark** — a business in a high-growth market but not the largest in it.
- **Cash cow** — the largest business in a low-growth market.
- **Dog** — a business in a low-growth market that is not the largest in it.

The Star Principle says:

- The best businesses are "stars": that is, they hold the number-one position in a market or niche that is growing fast (by at least 10 percent a year over several years).
- Stars are incredibly valuable because they can grow

exponentially, while also being very profitable and cash positive.

- Stars comprise only about one or two out of every hundred businesses, yet they account for more than 100 percent of cash generated over the lifetime of the product (because some non-star businesses absorb more cash than they generate). Hence stars are the businesses where entrepreneurs, venture capitalists, and other investors make all their money.

- It is possible to create a new star business by overtaking the early leader in your market, by inventing a whole new business category from scratch, or by re-segmenting into a new business category that is a subset of the original market.[1]

By applying the Star Principle to my investments I have built up my personal wealth.[2] Over the past twenty-three years I have invested in 16 startups or young companies, of which eight have returned at least five times my original capital. This has created returns of about 20 percent a year compounded — far above the average attained by professional venture capitalists.

How have I managed to do this? By following the Star Principle. I now invest only in businesses that are stars or have the potential to become stars in their particular markets.

There is, however, a problem. The Star Principle tells you whether an existing business is already a star. But it does not tell you how to *create* a star business, nor how to *overtake* the market leader in a high-growth market and thus become a star.

So is there another principle that can tell you how to do that, reliably and with a high chance of success?

I have spent the last four years trying to find out.

Working with the venture capitalist Greg Lockwood — my co-author on *Superconnect* — and supported by top-quality research from OC&C Strategy Consultants, I believe we have an answer. Dare I say, *the* answer?

And that answer is to *simplify* a business and a market.

If you wish to learn why that's so important, and how to do it, read on.

Preface

GREG LOCKWOOD

My job is to invest in businesses, so I am a professional sceptic. Instinctively, I dislike simplistic mantras and the latest management fad. I am predisposed to think that there is a lot of detail and nuance required to make businesses successful, and that the personalities who run a new company are all important. So, in many ways, I'm an odd co-conspirator with Richard, whose world-view is much more reductionist than my own — or that of just about anybody else I know!

Yet, during the fourteen years I've known Richard, he has helped me to understand that certain crude rules of thumb — while not invariably true — often contain concentrated insights and predictive power. The Star Principle and the 80/20 Principle are two well-validated examples. Richard's rules are always easy to grasp, easy to communicate and, perhaps most importantly, create the philosophical resolve that leads to action. In business, being *mostly correct and decisive* typically yields better results than taking the time to figure out what is perfectly correct.

The simplification of business, by reducing innovation to two alternative strategies — proven in practice — is a natural extension of Richard's 80/20 and Star principles. He simplifies the practice of strategy as well as the art of making businesses simple and highly effective.

A final attraction of the subject is that it deals with innovation in its most impactful sense. We often think of innovation as invention. There is rightly a cult of the inventor: after all, it takes a very special person to extend the bounds of knowledge, to create something fresh, or to conquer an unsolved problem. However, the first creation of knowledge touches few people. Those who deliver the most economic benefit to humanity are the simplifiers, the people who bring the fruits of invention and discovery to mass markets.

Benefit × People affected is when the world really changes, and where the highest economic rewards reside. The inventors deserve their pedestals. Equally, though, we should celebrate those who bring extraordinary value-for-money to millions. This is the cult of the simplifier.

The Secret Is Out!

In my Preface, I (Richard) talked about the importance of simplifying your business and your market. Why is this so desirable? Well, it turns out that it is the secret of creating a very large market, and of generating a very profitable business.

I first realized this when I was twenty-five and came across the Boston Consulting Group (BCG). I'd been to Wharton Business School, where I pursued an "individualized major," which was a fancy name for studying everything that interested me, including cooperatives, which were in vogue at the time but taught me nothing about creating a super-profitable business. In truth, I was in a bit of a panic as to who would employ me when I graduated, because I had not specialized in a narrow skill, such as corporate finance or marketing. Moreover, although I knew a lot of arcane things about business, I knew nothing that was particularly useful. So imagine my relief when I met the recruiters at BCG, who said that they were looking for young and frankly wet-behind-the-ears people like me, because they could train us using *their* model of business success, which involved categorizing a client's business as a star, a cash cow, a question mark or a dog, and then telling them what to do with it. I didn't need to know anything myself; I just had to learn how to do that kind of analysis.

Apart from relief, though, what struck me was what a really peculiar business BCG itself was. Here it was, charging some of the top companies in America and around the world a fortune for advice that could be mass produced by a handful of smart but totally inexperienced, newly minted MBAs. I came to discover that the work was very valuable to companies as they could sell or close firms with little potential, while concentrating on the few really good businesses that they had — the star businesses. Yet, what impressed me the most was how BCG could grow like billy-o and also generate extremely high margins because its own "costs of production" were so low. The simple principles behind the Boston Box made it possible for BCG to train almost unemployable people like me and then trust us to turn out original and useful analysis in a very short period of time.

How could BCG do this? *Because it simplified.* It boiled down the libraries of worthy work on business strategy into one dinky little model that could be replicated for any business at relatively low cost, but which could be sold at a very high price, because it had great benefits for the customers — the large industrial corporations that were BCG's market.

What were the benefits from the customer's viewpoint? The Boston Box was something that was so simple that it could be grasped by everyone throughout an organization, and so useful that it told all the firm's managers exactly what to do. It was easy to use, highly practical, elegant, and memorable. It could be used as a simplifying and unifying communication device throughout the client organization.

> Is your business a star? Get your Star Principle
> score in sixty seconds at www.simplify.fm.

That set me thinking that perhaps the most successful companies were ones that were not only the market leaders in a high-growth market (the Star Principle), but also the most simple. In hard economic terms, simplifying has two great benefits:

- it can lead to high growth in a business and market; and
- it can do so at high margins, because simplifying can lead to low costs of production and high prices at the same time.

What a neat trick to pull!

Throughout my career, I had always been on the lookout for simple answers, but I had never applied the principle template to simplifying in the same systematic way as I had with the 80/20 and Star principles. Then, about five years ago, Greg pointed out this gap in my thinking. That was how we started the journey that culminated in the book you are holding in your hands.

The Secret Red Thread

Greg and I came to the conclusion that simplifying *should* lead to extraordinary success. But there was a big surprise in store for us. We decided that the best way to illustrate simplifying — and to identify *how* to simplify — would be to explore case studies of the most successful simplifiers of the past hundred years or so. This was easier than we expected. There were plenty of great case studies available to us, from both the distant and the very recent past.

Then the truth dawned on us — the real secret of simplifying: Nearly all of the great success stories of the twentieth century — right up to the present day — are stories of simplifying.

We discovered that simplifying not only *should* lead to great economic success — as the theories of strategy and economics suggest. By observing men and women who have changed not only the face of business but how we work and live, we also learned that clever and creative simplifying *has and continues* to do just that. It really does lead to extraordinary success, and it has a huge impact on society to boot.

If you make a list of the people who have been most successful in the last hundred years — or, if you prefer, the last fifty, twenty, ten or even five years — a large majority of them have been great simplifiers:

- Henry Ford;
- Allen Lane;
- the McDonald Brothers and Ray Kroc;
- Walt Disney;
- Ingvar Kamprad;
- Kihachiro Kawashima;
- Bruce Henderson;
- F. Kenneth Iverson;
- Herb Kelleher;
- Steve Jobs and Jony Ive;
- Akio Morita;
- Bill Bain;

- James Dyson;
- Mitt Romney;
- Jeff Bezos;
- Pierre Omidyar;
- Larry Page and Sergey Brin;
- Daniel Ek;
- Joe Gebbia; and
- Travis Kalanick and Garrett Camp.

The list goes on and on, and it continues to grow as new "unicorns" (private companies valued at more than a billion dollars) emerge every month.

All of these entrepreneurs simplified. Some of them were quite upfront about it. For instance, Henry Ford said of his revolutionary new car, the Model T, that

"... its most important feature was its simplicity ... I thought it was up to me as the designer to make the car so completely simple that no one could fail to understand it. That works both ways and applies to everything. The less complex an article, the easier it is to make, the cheaper it may be sold, and therefore the greater number may be sold."[1]

Ray Kroc wrote that the McDonald brothers had created

"... a radically different kind of operation, a restaurant stripped down to the minimum in service and menu, the prototype for legions of fast-food units that would later spread across the land ... Of course, the simplicity of the procedure allowed the McDonalds to concentrate on quality in every step, and that was the trick. When I saw it working that day in 1954, I felt like some latter-day Newton who'd just had an Idaho potato caromed off his skull."[2]

His first motto for McDonald's, he said, "was KISS, which meant, Keep it simple, stupid."

Steve Jobs described his whole approach as "very simple ... the way we're running the company, the product design, the advertising, it all comes down to this: Let's make it simple. Really simple."[3] His biographer, Walter Isaacson, wrote that Jobs "made devices simpler by eliminating buttons, software simpler by eliminating features, and interfaces simpler by eliminating options. He attributed his love of simplicity to his Zen training."[4] Jony Ive, the creator of every Apple device from the iPod onwards, constantly harps on to anyone who will listen that his approach is to make products that are incredibly simple to use, even though the design process itself is extremely difficult. He stresses that it is hard to make something so simple. His task, he says, is "to solve incredibly complex problems and make their resolution appear inevitable and incredibly simple, so that you have no sense of how difficult this thing was."[5]

Given these clues, Greg and I find it extraordinary that, so far as we can tell, nobody has previously realized that simplifying is *the* key to the kind of product and business innovation that creates incredibly high value for customers, society and shareholders alike. Simplifying has been an invisible red thread running through business history in our lifetime, and that of our parents and grandparents.

But now the secret is out! And this should enable tens of thousands of new innovators — perhaps you are one of them — to create extraordinary value for themselves and others.

The process of intelligent innovation can be speeded up!

Not only that, Greg and I have made another discovery. All of these simplifiers — every single one — followed one of just two simplifying approaches. So if you want to know *how* to simplify, our answer is that you have a choice of two equally reliable and well-validated models.

How to Simplify

The two simplifying strategies are quite different and nearly always incompatible. So, as we'll show through multiple examples, if you want to simplify, you must choose just one of them. After some reflection and a few tests, which we will explain in detail later, it will become clear which of the two strategies is better suited to your venture, aspirations and market opportunity. You must then be uncompromising in executing the chosen strategy.

The strategies themselves are simple.

The first we call *price-simplifying*. This requires cutting the price of a product or service in half, or more. Sometimes, within a few years, prices may be cut by 90 percent. On the face of it, this might sound unrealistic. Yet we will show you numerous examples of when it has happened. The new — hugely cheaper — product or service is not identical to the old, expensive product, but it fulfills the same basic function. For example, no one would argue that traveling on a budget airline is as pleasant an experience as traveling on a full-service rival, but they still get you from A to B quickly and safely. And yet, as we will explain, the way to cut prices by 50–90 percent is usually *not* to provide an inferior product, but rather to organize the delivery of the product in a different way that allows much higher volume and greater efficiency ... and often to co-opt the customers into doing some of the work!

In a nutshell, price-simplifying works because markets usually respond to dramatic price cuts by multiplying their size exponentially. If the price is halved, demand does not double. It increases fivefold, tenfold, a hundredfold, a thousandfold or more. If prices are reduced to a fifth or a tenth of what they were originally, demand may multiply by ten thousand or a hundred thousand times. Occasionally, the multiples may be measured in the millions — look at what McDonald's did to the hamburger market.

Yet price-simplifying makes financial sense only if you are able to make the product simpler to make and thereby cut costs by at least half.

Of course, it is not easy to halve costs and prices, let alone drive them down to a tenth of what they were. But there is a reliable template for doing this. Even better, it works equally well in every industry and region of the world. Price-simplifying can involve radical redesign not only of a product but also of the way that the industry is organized — what is called in the jargon *business system redesign*. To stand a whole industry on its head is hard. Still, there is a reliable way to transform the industry, common to nearly all the examples in our research.

Video by Richard Koch: How price simplifiers exponentially spike demand, creating markets that did not exist before: www.simplify.fm.

Our term for the second strategy, which is very different but equally effective, is *proposition-simplifying*. This involves creating a product that is useful, appealing, and very easy to use, such as the iPad (or any other Apple device of the last decade), the Vespa scooter, the Google search engine or the Uber taxi app. Proposition-simplified products are also usually aesthetically pleasing.

Proposition-simplifying creates a large market that did not previously exist in the same form, or at all. For instance, there was no market for tablet computers before the iPad. Unlike price-simplifying, products that proposition-simplify do not involve a radical reduction in price; they may even command a price premium. Yet proposition-simplifying also multiplies value for money and therefore market size by making the product or service so much easier to use as well as more practical and/or beautiful. Proposition-simplifying works when the product becomes a *joy to use*.

As with price-simplifying, there is a common formula for how to proposition-simplify, and we will explain it to you.

If you are the impatient type — and impatience is a virtue in business — and want to jump straight to our conclusions, feel free to go directly to Part Four: The Rewards of Simplifying, which lays out the research and summarizes our most important findings. Then read the whole book later.

For the more patient, linear reader — and patience is also a virtue — we suggest starting at the beginning, with Part One: Great Simplifiers, which describes a dozen standout cases of successful simplifying.

Part Two: How to Simplify will help you decide which of the two simplifying strategies is better for you and your firm, and then provides a template for each.

Part Three — provocatively titled Save the Dinosaurs? — examines the threat to established market leaders from simplifiers and how leading firms can stay on top. For an interactive guide to simplifying and how it can help established businesses, visit www.SIMPLIFYforCEOs.com.

Part Four: The Rewards of Simplifying looks at the financial rewards that have been gained by simplifiers in their respective fields, as examined independently of the two authors by an elite firm of strategy consultants. OC&C selected and analyzed twelve cases, six of each type of simplifying. Greg and I then explain why these companies have been so successful and how the case studies resemble — or contrast with — each other.

Visit www.simplify.fm and www.SIMPLIFYforCEOs.com for more online tools.

PART ONE

Great Simplifiers

We start by looking at some of the best examples of simplifying that our research uncovered. There are plenty of recent examples of great simplifying, but we also present quite a few cases that date back many decades. Some of you may question the value of "ancient" business history. But we would turn the question around and ask, "Where are we likely to find the simplifiers who have had the most impact on the world?" Admittedly, some of these are relatively modern — Apple, Google, eBay, Amazon.com, and we believe that Uber will make it into that pantheon before long. But other examples, such as Ford and McDonald's, started a long time ago. As we will see, the most valuable simplifiers are often those that have proven track records of growth and staying power over many decades. Their successful methods have been followed by more recent simplifiers . . . and you can follow, too.

1

The Man Who
Democratized Travel

The ordinary way of doing business is not the best way.

Henry Ford

Ancient history? No one in business today can remember the earthquake caused by Henry Ford, and even in business schools his case is rarely taught. Yet we will see that Ford's story has priceless lessons for any ambitious entrepreneur or executive today.

When he was 45, and a moderately successful industrialist, Henry Ford took a brave stand that shook the world. The decision not only created his fortune but made him a leading architect of the twentieth century and one of the most celebrated and influential people on the planet.

He decided to simplify and democratize the automobile.

> Video by Richard Koch: How Henry Ford's Simplifying
> vision eclipsed all others in the car industry:
> www.simplify.fm.

Ford recalled the turning-point in his autobiography:

"What I am trying to emphasize is that the ordinary way of doing business is not the best way. I am coming to the point of my entire departure from the ordinary methods. From this point dates the extraordinary success of the company.

We had been fairly following the custom of the trade. Our automobile was less complex than any other. We had no outside money in the concern. But aside from these two points we did not differ materially from the other automobile companies."[1]

When Ford had his light-bulb moment, several hundred rival entrepreneurs were making cars. They were much the same in background and activity: all engineers; nearly all product designers; all auto enthusiasts, entering cars in motor races and taking a keen interest in who won; and all making no more than a few cars a day. They sold them to the same type of customer, too — the only market at that time for cars — rich and leisured gentlemen, usually motor "nuts," skilled in driving and maintaining their beautiful beasts. Ford, though not the market leader, was one of the biggest manufacturers, making around five vehicles a day.

But however conventional he appeared in 1908, there was always something odd about Henry Ford and his opinions. "From the day the first motor car appeared on the streets," he wrote, "it had to me appeared to be a necessity."[2] This was considered an eccentric view at a time when the cost of a car was far more than the annual wages of a skilled worker. Yet Ford was a stubborn man. Though his whole industry was in the business of providing "pleasure cars" for the rich, Ford conceived a vision of something completely different. To their horror, he told his salespeople:

"I will build a motor car for the great multitude. It will be large enough for the family but small enough for the individual to run and care for. It will be constructed of the best materials, by the best men to be hired, after the simplest designs that modern engineering can devise. But it will be so low in price that no man making a good salary would be unable to own one — and enjoy with his family the blessing of hours of pleasure in God's great open spaces."[3]

This vision, he said, "led me to build to one end — a car that would meet the wants of the multitude ... year following year, the pressure was, and still is, to improve and refine, and make better, with an increasing reduction in price."[4]

The idea of democratizing the automobile inspired Ford. His great insight was that the key was price. If he could make a car cheap enough, it would, he believed, sell in vast quantities. He had some supporting evidence: in 1905–6, Ford made two models, one priced at $1,000 and the other at $2,000. The company sold 1599 cars that year. The following year he simplified both models and slashed the prices: "The big thing was that [my] cheapest car sold for $600 and the most expensive for only $750, and right there came the complete demonstration of what price meant. We sold 8,423 cars, nearly five times as many as in our previous biggest year."[5]

It's all very well to realize that price might be the key to expanding sales, but how did Ford manage to keep his prices sufficiently low to create a new mass market? His first idea was to redesign the product and make just one standardized, simple model:

"Therefore in 1909 I announced one morning, without any previous warning, that in future we were going to build only one model, that the model was going to be the 'Model T,' and that the chassis would be exactly the same for all cars ...'[6]

The most important feature of the new model ... was its simplicity. There were but four constructional units in the car — the power plant, the frame, the front axle, and the rear axle ... I thought it was up to me as the designer to make the car so completely simple that no one could fail to understand it.

That works both ways and applies to everything. The less complex an article, the easier it is to make, the cheaper it may be sold, and therefore the greater number may be sold."[7]

So, by making a single product — for more than a decade, with few variations and options permitted — Ford could reduce his costs considerably.

He also paid great attention to the materials that went into his cars. For example, he pioneered the use of vanadium steel, a French invention that was both very light and very strong — ideal to create usefulness for the customer. There were initial difficulties to overcome: no steel maker in America could manufacture it. So Ford found a small company in Canton, Ohio, and covered the cost of the early trials himself. As he recounted, "the first heat was a failure. Very little vanadium remained in the steel. I had them try again, and the second time the steel came through."[8] The new product had a tensile strength of 170,000, about 260 percent that of normal American steel. The vanadium steel disposed of most of the weight in Ford's car — decreasing fuel consumption — yet actually cost less than the traditional alternative.

The other plank of Ford's low-price car was a new production system, geared to make vehicles at high scale and low cost. He built the world's biggest factory — not just the biggest *car* factory — on a massive sixty-acre site at Highland Park, near Detroit. It opened on New Year's Day, 1910, and the gain in productivity was marked: "Contrast the year 1908 with the year 1911 … The average number of employees [rose] from 1,908 to 4,110, and the cars built from a little over six thousand to nearly thirty-five thousand. You will note that men were not employed in proportion to the output."[9]

However, although Ford managed to increase the number of cars produced per employee by nearly three times in just three years, and his cars became much cheaper to make than those of any of his rivals, the absolute level of efficiency remained low. The real breakthrough came with a proprietary innovation, designed by his production managers: the move from batch production to a continuously moving assembly line. This didn't happen until 1913, and it was then that Ford famously insisted that all of his cars would be painted black, because only Japan black paint could dry quickly enough to keep up with the speed of the line.

The effect of simplification and scale was to move the price of a Model T down to $550 by 1914, when 248,307 of them were sold. By 1917, the price had fallen even further, to $360, with the result that sales soared to 785,432. In 1920, 1.25 million Model T's were bought. Compared to 1909, a price reduction of 63 percent — to almost a third of the original price of the Model T, which was itself a good fifth cheaper than comparable cars — had resulted in a sixty-sevenfold increase in the number of cars Ford sold.

Compared to Ford's sales in 1905–6 (the year before the simplifying strategy began), the sales in 1920 marked a 781-times increase. Simplifying made the company's cars both easier and cheaper to make. And the price reduction was enormously effective in boosting the whole market as well as Ford's share of it. By 1920, his share had soared to 56 percent, three times larger than that of his nearest rival, General Motors, which was an agglomeration of five different car brands. Ford was by far the most profitable car company in the world, both absolutely — relative to sales — and relative to capital employed.

Even Henry Ford himself was surprised by how much demand responded to the lower price. A price reduction to 35–40 percent of the original price boosted sales by more than 700 times. We shall see this pattern repeated throughout this book — the impact of a really chunky price reduction on sales is always grossly underestimated. The relationship between price reduction and demand expansion is asymmetrical. If you cut price by half or more, demand rises *exponentially* — by tens or hundreds or thousands of times. This is one of our most important findings. Radical cost reduction is one of the most powerful economic forces in the universe.

Henry Ford is our first price-simplifier. His overriding objective was to cut the price of his cars dramatically — to well below a half of the previous level. His case perfectly illustrates how cost and price reduction is not a one-off affair, but a gradual, continual process, fuelled by a few big innovations — in Ford's case a simplified car model, standardizing on one model, and the moving assembly line — and a mass of smaller ones. Prices don't have to be slashed in half immediately. Instead, a virtuous circle can be created, where the first cost reductions create a larger market and greater market share, with the benefits of greater scale subsequently lowering costs and prices, and raising demand further. What is essential, however, is a dogged commitment to achieve the lowest possible cost and price.

Though Ford's main objective in simplifying was always to cut costs, he also simplified to achieve two other objectives — a more useful car (higher utility) and one that was easier to drive and maintain (greater ease of use). One reason why the Model T was more useful was that it used a new grade of steel that was both stronger and lighter than earlier versions. As a result, Ford's car was both more rugged and more economical to run than its rivals — fuel consumption rises with weight. He designed the car for "simplicity in operation — because the masses are not mechanics,"[10] introducing a "planetary transmission" that made the gears easy to change and the car easy to maneuver. Hence the slogan "Anybody can drive a Ford." Because the car was simplified into four structural units (the power plant, the frame, and the front and rear axles), and these were easily accessible, no special skill was required to repair or replace broken parts.

All of these design changes combined lower cost with greater utility and ease of use. Specifically, Ford's cars were lighter, cheaper to run and maintain, more rugged and reliable, and easier to drive, maintain, and repair.

Results

- For Henry Ford, a personal fortune estimated by *Forbes* in 2008 at $188 billion (in 2008 dollars), most of which he bequeathed to the Ford Foundation. Ford also invented the American answer to Marxism — "Fordism:" the mass production of simple, well-designed, cheap products, combined with high wages for workers. After the success of the Model T, Ford was courted by U.S. presidents and he even influenced, for good and ill, the industrial policies of Lenin, Stalin, and Hitler.
- For the Ford Motor Company, the creation of a powerful brand that has survived egregious mismanagement (including under Henry Ford himself and his son Edsel). The company has lasted over 110 years and currently is valued at $59 billion, having grown in value each year since 1906 by nearly 10 percent compounded.[11]
- The creation of a huge global mass market for cars.
- Greater freedom for the mass of people resulting from personal mobility, previously enjoyed only by the privileged few.
- Ford foreshadowed some of the other great simplifiers who are discussed in this book, because they built on his methods.

Key Points

1. One way to create a huge new market — with a different type of customer, only able or willing to pay a much lower price — is to simplify your product so that it is much easier and cheaper to make, and hence sell.
2. In order to price-simplify, you need to reduce the price by at least 50 percent. This does not need to happen all at once, but you need to continue cutting costs and prices each year — by about 10 percent a year.
3. Take a lesson from Ford:

   - Redesign your product from first principles, cutting out unnecessary or costly parts.
   - Reduce product-line variety and if possible standardize on a single "universal product."
   - Reduce the number of components.
   - Eliminate frills and unnecessary options.
   - Use different, new, lighter, and cheaper materials.
   - Go for volume and production facilities that are far larger than those of your rivals.
   - Organize tasks to maximize the specialization of your workforce.
   - Automate tasks.

4. If you are a price-simplifier, cutting your prices is the primary objective. But, like Ford, also increase your product's quality, utility, and ease of use if this can be done without incurring extra costs.

2

The Billionaire Who
Travels by Bus

Reach good results with small means.

Ingvar Kamprad

Ingvar Kamprad has furnished more rooms than anyone else, living or dead. He built up a company from nothing to being worth more than $40 billion. And he has done it all by simplifying.

Ingvar Kamprad was only seventeen when he founded IKEA as a mail-order company. Five years later he started selling furniture. The story goes that one day he couldn't fit a table into his car, and a friend suggested removing the legs. Kamprad immediately had the idea of flat-packed furniture.[1] He realized that half the sale price of a table was in the cost of transporting it. So if he could persuade the customer to do the final assembly — by engineering parts that fitted together easily and providing unambiguous instructions — he could cut his costs in half. It was a true epiphany.

The firm's purpose is to sell stylish furniture at low prices. In 1976 Kamprad wrote *The Testament of a Furniture Dealer*, his firm's Bible.[2] The book stresses simplicity as the means to provide furniture at prices that are not just unbeatable but astounding. Yes, IKEA products should look good; yes, they should be as stylish as possible; yes, the firm builds extensively on the Swedish heritage of informal quality. But make no mistake, IKEA is founded on the idea that its goods should cost no more than half — and preferably a third — the price of equivalent furniture and furnishings. For example, in 1996, the company wanted to sell a mug for five kronor (about 40 pence or 55 U.S. cents). A large part of the cost was transportation, so IKEA found a way to fit 864 mugs on a single pallet. Even then, the cost was deemed too high, so the mug was redesigned in order to fit 1280 on each pallet. Eventually, through further redesigns, 2024 mugs could be loaded on to a pallet, reducing shipping costs by 60 percent.[3]

The obsession with target prices and economy comes directly from IKEA's founder. Employees still talk about the time Kamprad attended a glittering event to collect a Businessman of the Year award. The security guards saw him arrive by bus and refused to let him in.[4]

How Can IKEA Be So Much Cheaper?

Much of the answer lies in those transportation costs. Consider that a table or a bookcase sold through a shop has to be transported at least twice and often three times — from the factory to a warehouse; from there to the store; then from the store to the customer's home. IKEA eliminates most of this cost. Typically, its goods travel only once at IKEA's expense — from the manufacturer to the store. And because the goods are in flat packs, they are much easier and cheaper to transport and to store than pre-assembled furniture. Of course, *somebody* then has to take the product to the customer's home and assemble it there. But that person is the customer! We'll come shortly to why customers are happy to do this.

First, though, we need to look at what else IKEA does to make its prices so attractive? If all there was to IKEA was flat-pack furniture, it would be easy to imitate. Indeed, many other stores now sell flat-pack furniture. But none has come close to emulating IKEA's scale, success or rock-bottom prices. Why is that?

Part of the answer lies in the giant stores that IKEA has built on the edges of cities. These are far larger than its rivals' equivalents in all of the countries where it operates. Another part of the answer is the way it organizes its stores. Right from the beginning, the stores were massive and featured a novel way of enticing customers past their wares — what IKEA cheekily calls "the long natural way." This involves a steady progression, as though in a theme park, anticlockwise through the store. There are a lot of product categories, but relatively few products within each category. Instead of asking a salesperson for advice, customers must choose for themselves, helped by clear instructions, placards and a very well-designed, mass-produced catalog. They then take their purchases on a cart or in a bag to the checkout, and from there they take them home.

IKEA therefore obtains for itself and its customers five further cost benefits, over and above the transport cost savings:

- One-stop shopping. IKEA covers just about every category of goods you need to furnish a home, from bedding and cushions to artworks. This is convenient for customers and also increases sales.
- High sales per store, even relative to space, combined with lower premises costs as a result of being located outside the city center.
- Low cost of sales staff as there are very few of them.
- High sales per product stocked, by stocking a relatively limited range within each product category. The mugs may be cheap and cheerful, but don't expect a huge choice of them.
- By testing new designs in a few stores first, IKEA works out which lines will work and which will not, so it doesn't order large quantities of goods that won't sell and will have to be discounted (a common bugbear in the furniture trade).

Yet that is not all. At the heart of IKEA's simple system is a different way of organizing its industry. IKEA is a retailer, but it also designs most of its furniture and selects its manufacturing partners carefully, giving them very large orders for only a few products. This lowers the furniture-makers' costs dramatically; it also raises IKEA's bargaining power. The manufacturers become part of the IKEA system.

The all-encompassing IKEA system is a lot simpler and more efficient than the traditional way of producing and selling furniture, which comprises a patchwork of mainly small furniture-makers, selling to small chains of retailers, with the difficult job of moving products to retail outlets sometimes handled by the manufacturers' own small transport systems, but mainly contracted out to third-party logistics firms that are not specialists in furniture. Before IKEA came along, the furniture industry was a mess — highly complex and sub-scale in all three stages (production, retail, and distribution), with poor coordination across these stages.

Ingvar Kamprad gradually reconstructed the whole industry, just as Henry Ford did with the car industry. Both men developed *new business systems* that offered customers a much better deal — much lower prices and better value for money — by making their industries hugely more efficient. Cars and furniture are obviously very different products, yet there are common elements in what Ford and Kamprad did, elements that you can emulate if there is a chance to reconstruct your own industry:

- Simple product design to eliminate unnecessary costs.
- Limited product variety within each category, so more of each product line can be made and sold; as a result, stock-keeping costs are decimated.
- Much greater scale.
- Great reduction in cost at every stage of production and distribution. In Ford's case, this was achieved through the assembly line, whereas Kamprad organized the functional equivalent of an assembly line within his stores, with the customer doing most of the "assembly," both in the store and at home.
- The beauty of Ford and Kamprad's systems was that

they became *proprietary* — peculiar to their own organization, excluding rivals. Once Ford had built the biggest factory in the world, there wasn't space in the market for anyone else to follow suit. Once Kamprad had built his stores, nobody else could copy his system — the market in each location and overall was just not big enough. If he had moved too slowly, and an imitator had managed to out-IKEA IKEA by building a similar but larger system, Kamprad's company would have foundered. But nobody did. The charm of his new business system was the way it all fitted together. Once rivals really understood how it worked, it was too late for them to imitate it.

How IKEA Seduces Its Customers

IKEA would not make so much money without getting its customers to lend a hand. So how does it manage to convince those customers to do so much hard work? And why do they put up with it?

A very low price — less than half the price under the traditional system — is the obvious answer. This is also the correct answer. But it is not the whole answer.

If price were IKEA's only appeal, it would have far fewer customers. If you walk through an IKEA store, you will see not only hard-up students and young married couples, but also plenty of well-heeled people. You don't even need to go into the store — just wander around the parking lot and you'll see plenty of Volvos and 4x4s and BMWs, not to mention a small number of Bentleys and Jags. But you may need to go into the store to understand why. If you look at the shoppers' experience, you'll soon realize that, although IKEA asks a lot of its customers, it gives back a lot too — advantages you won't find in a typical furniture store.

IKEA increases the *usefulness* of its products and its shopping experience by offering a one-stop solution. A visit to the store can be a day out for the whole family — there are play areas for children, and inexpensive restaurants.

Then there is the *art* embodied in the products. We define art as anything that is emotionally appealing or attractive that cannot be reduced to hard economic usefulness. IKEA's products meet this definition by being well designed and stylish.

IKEA also increases *ease of use* for its customers. The stores are easy to find — with their colossal yellow-and-blue signs — and have ample, free parking. There is a more extensive range of stock sitting within the store than elsewhere. And the vast majority of items can be taken away immediately — no waiting for delivery.

For many customers, these advantages of shopping at IKEA — quite apart from the low prices — balance or even outweigh the disadvantages (mainly the time and effort that the IKEA system demands). But this is where Ingvar Kamprad was particularly cunning. If you scrutinize the non-price advantages, you notice one thing in common: *they are all either relatively cheap to provide or even generate extra profits for IKEA.* A few jugglers or magicians across a large crowd don't cost very much per head, and if they draw in a few more families they more than pay for themselves. The restaurants make a profit. If the play area for children encourages a young couple to stay longer in the store, they will likely end up spending more. Good design costs no more than bad design. Signage serves as cheap advertising, usually seen from a nearby motorway or main road. The land on which each store is built is usually cheap, often bought in an area where there are no neighboring shops, so the parking lots don't cost much. There's plenty of stock in the stores, yet because they attract a huge flow of customers, inventory is actually higher than in traditional stores.

While it offers these low-cost (or profit-making) benefits to its customers, IKEA has deliberately chosen *not* to provide certain typical — high-cost — industry services. For instance, if IKEA had lots of well-paid salespeople swanning around its stores, the cost would bite badly into profits. If the furniture was not self-assembly, its cost would almost double. One of Ingvar Kamprad's key principles is "Reach good results with small means ... We have no interest in a solution until we know what it costs."[5]

Like Ford, Kamprad was a price-simplifier. A common tactic in price-simplifying is to cut back certain expensive services and to compensate for this by lavishly providing low-cost (or, ideally, profit-making) services. As we've seen, that is exactly what IKEA does.

The overriding objective is to cut prices yet offer "cheap" or "free" benefits to draw in more customers. These benefits can be categorized as *ease of use*, *greater usefulness*, and *art*. These provide a template for any simplifier to dream up cheap or free advantages for their customers. The other principal weapons in the simplifier's armory are ingenuity, scale, seeing the business from the customers' perspective (IKEA is very good at this), customer segmentation (selecting the target market carefully and knowing who is within it and who is outside it), and being extremely hard-nosed about cutting any non-essential features that cost extra or complicate the business system.

Yet the big test of any new system for a simplifying firm over the long term is whether it can be imitated or improved by a rival. If the new business system is bold enough, if it eliminates traditional benefits that the customer is willing to forgo in exchange for large price cuts, and if it provides other benefits that are both cheap and unique, then the risk of imitation or supersession falls dramatically. Market share provides the final bulwark against this risk. If, like IKEA, you can win more than half of the relevant market (self-assembly furniture, in IKEA's case), and be ten times larger than any rival, you are likely to be secure unless a rival spots a different way to discount prices again. In IKEA's case, this seems highly unlikely.

Results

- IKEA invented the flat-pack furniture market and has provided elegant, inexpensive furniture to tens of millions of customers.
- IKEA is the world's largest furniture retailer, with annual sales in the region of 29 billion euros. In its core European markets, IKEA is nearly ten times larger than its nearest rival.
- While the industry has grown by 2 percent per year, IKEA's growth has been 14 percent.
- IKEA is highly profitable, with operating margins over 15 percent — more than double the rest of the industry. We estimate that the company is worth $47 billion.

Key Points

1. IKEA proves that, with imagination and the right template, prices can be more than halved — in its case by between 50 and 80 percent.

2. Ingvar Kamprad constructed a new business system based on self-assembly of furniture, stylish product design, giant stores, massive volume of sales per product line, and control of third-party manufacturers, who were integrated into the IKEA system. Can you think of a new business system for your industry that could enable you to cut prices by more than 50 percent?

3. IKEA integrated its customers into the production and retailing system, persuading them to do much of the work. Again, is there a parallel with your own industry, or could there be?

4. Customers play ball not just because of extremely low prices but also because IKEA offers them advantages and an experience that other retailers do not. Are there ways in which your firm — or a new venture — could offer customers advantages that would not cost you very much, or would even increase profits?

5. IKEA's system now appears to be impregnable because the firm's market share and very high sales levels protect it from imitators. This was not inevitable, however: if a quick-thinking rival had been fast enough to imitate IKEA's system and implemented it outside Sweden. So, if you invent a way of price-simplifying that works, be sure to roll it out internationally before local rivals have a chance to copy it.

3

The Assembly Line of Food

*A designer knows he has achieved
perfection not when there is nothing left
to add, but when there is nothing
left to take away.*

Antoine de Saint-Exupéry[1]

Three men created this golden icon, which is recognized and loved (and hated) around the globe. Simplifying can work just as well in service industries as for products, and for precisely the same reasons.

One day in 1954, a fifty-two-year-old man, not in the best of health, flew from Chicago to Los Angeles. The following day, bright and early, he drove sixty miles towards the Mojave Desert. His destination was a small, octagonal building, located on a corner in a small town. The stranger was not impressed by the humble structure. It did not seem to fit with what he had heard.

Shortly before eleven o'clock, employees began to file in — men dressed in spiffy white shirts, smart trousers, and paper hats. The stranger liked that. The men began to trundle trolleys laden with food and drinks into the building, their tempo picking up so much that they reminded the stranger of ants bustling around a picnic. Cars began to arrive, the parking lot soon filled up, and lines began to form as customers stepped up to the windows.

The investigator was impressed by the activity, but still dubious. He joined the line and said to the man in front of him — swarthy but well dressed, in a seersucker suit — "Say, what's the attraction here?"

"Never eaten here before?"

"Nope."

"Well, you'll see. You'll get the best hamburger you ever ate for just fifteen cents. And you don't have to mess around with tipping waitresses."

The stranger left the line to walk around the corner, where he found several workers sitting in the shade, gnawing on hamburgers. He approached a man in a carpenter's apron and asked him how often he came there for lunch.

"Every damn day," he said without a pause in his munching. "Sure beats the old lady's cold meatloaf sandwiches."[2]

The stranger was Ray Kroc, a dogged drink-machine salesman. After the lunchtime rush, he introduced himself to the drive-in restaurant's bosses, Mac and Dick McDonald, and arranged to take them out to dinner.

As the brothers outlined their system that evening, Kroc became hooked by its simplicity and efficiency. The menu was strictly limited to just nine items, including drinks. The food comprised of either hamburgers or cheeseburgers and fries. The burgers were all identical — a tenth of a pound of beef, all cooked the same way. Whereas a coffee shop sold a hamburger for thirty cents, it was only fifteen at McDonald's, or four cents more for a cheeseburger. The star attraction was the French fries, though — another bargain at ten cents for a three-ounce bag. The menu was completed by coffee at a nickel a cup, soft drinks at a dime, or a large milkshake for twenty cents. That was it.

Kroc had tracked down a remarkable unsung success story in San Bernardino. The brothers had started their business back in 1948, when they turned the barbecue restaurant they'd been running into a slick assembly-line operation they called a "speedee service line." At the time the typical mass-market restaurant was a mom-and-pop coffee shop offering hundreds of items. The brothers' nine-item menu never changed. Food was always cooked and served in the same automated way, so customers always got their meals immediately, when they were hot. They paid when they ordered, and cleared away their own debris after eating.

All of the food was good, especially the fries, yet Kroc stressed that the main attraction was the price. A meal at McDonald's cost about half the equivalent at a coffee shop. How had Dick and Mac McDonald managed to do this?

Like Henry Ford and Ingvar Kamprad, they added value by subtraction. By removing menu variety, they made it much simpler to procure ingredients, operate the restaurant, and cook and serve the food. They subtracted waitresses. By simplifying and automating the whole pro-cess, persuading customers to do some of the work, and producing assembly-line food, their labor costs per serving were reduced to a fraction of those of a typical coffee shop. The levels of throughput were astounding, too. The little shop that Ray Kroc visited had sales exceeding $400,000 a year (around $4 million in today's money) — more than that of an average (much bigger) McDonald's today.[3]

By sourcing beef and other ingredients in large quantities, a virtuous circle was created — lower prices for hamburgers, leading to higher demand, further increasing purchasing muscle and overhead cost coverage, resulting in yet-lower prices but also higher margins. Even when it was a tiny operation with just a handful of restaurants, McDonald's had great purchasing power, which allowed it to cut costs. The restaurants needed to buy fewer than forty items in total to make their nine products, unlike a coffee shop which needed to purchase hundreds of items for its far more extensive menu. Even with sales no greater than those of the local coffee shop, therefore, each McDonald's outlet had much more concentrated buying power for its buns, ketchup, mustard, and other ingredients.[4]

Kroc recognized a money-making machine when he saw it. He also realized that the way to achieve even lower costs, and therefore prices, was to scale up the operation, while maintaining its pristine simplicity. At dinner that first day with the brothers, he told them that he'd never seen anything to rival their system in all the time he'd been selling milkshake machines to restaurants and drive-ins throughout America. He asked the McDonalds why they hadn't already opened dozens of outlets and was met by silence. "I felt like I'd dragged my tie in my soup or something. The two brothers just sat there looking at me."[5]

Finally, Mac turned round to point up a hill that rose behind the restaurant. There was a big white house with a large and pretty porch, from where the McDonalds could watch the sunset. They loved the peace and quiet and didn't want the hassle of expansion. They were happy with their lot.

Kroc didn't understand. He felt they were sitting on a gold mine, and if he were in their position . . .

What had the McDonalds achieved before they met Kroc? They had invented a product and proved its potential. They had reinvented the restaurant and proved the economics of fast-food simplicity. The good deal for the customer and its attraction were also basically in place. As with Ford and IKEA, the overwhelming attraction was dramatically lower prices. The original huge sign hanging over the first restaurant proclaimed "McDonald's famous Hamburgers — Buy by the Bag," but this was framed on both left and right by a simple "15c" in far bigger point size. Fifteen cents.[6]

In addition, there were subsidiary benefits (again, as with both Ford and IKEA):

1. Usefulness:

   - High-quality food. As Ray Kroc said, "the simplicity of the procedure allowed the McDonald's to concentrate on quality in every step, and that was the trick."[7]
   - Consistency and reliability — an identical product time after time.

2. Art:

   - Spiffy uniforms for sharp employees.
   - The Golden Arches.

26   PART 1 • THE ASSEMBLY LINE OF FOOD

- Cleanliness and visible hygiene in the store.
- The McDonald's name and "M" branding.

3. Ease of use:

- Fast service.
- No tipping.

The brothers licensed eight other outlets in California and two in Arizona, but these restaurants failed to adopt the simplified approach of the San Bernardino operation. According to Ray Kroc, "The brothers" own store in San Bernardino was virtually the only "pure" McDonald's operation. Others had adulterated the menu with things like pizza, burritos, and enchiladas. In many of them the quality of the hamburgers was inferior, because they were grinding hearts into the meat and the high fat content made it greasy."[8]

Kroc had the vision of a host of "pure" McDonald's franchisees. He negotiated a deal with the brothers whereby he would franchise the new outlets, and in 1961 he bought the whole company for $2.7 million (about $21 million in today's money).

Then he set about turning McDonald's into a big chain. He created a universal product of high quality, and produced a uniform system that allowed no variation, making it sufficiently simple to be franchised to thousands of entrepreneurs while still retaining absolute control and consistency. In his short memoir, he devotes a full twelve pages to the beauty of McDonald's fries, which he claims are in a different league to those of their rivals and prepared with religious devotion, both under the brothers and on a far bigger scale under his stewardship.

Initially, getting the French fries right on an industrial scale was one of Kroc's biggest challenges. He describes the dismay he felt in 1955 when he opened his first franchise restaurant in Des Plaines, Illinois, and failed to replicate the taste of the McDonald brothers' fries. His fries, he said, were as good as elsewhere, but they were not a patch on the McDonalds' fries in California. Hugely frustrated, he called the brothers, but they couldn't work out what he was doing wrong. The breakthrough came when a researcher at the Potato and Onion Association asked Kroc to describe in detail the procedure for making fries in San Bernardino. The secret turned out to be that the potatoes were stored in open chicken-wire shaded bins, which allowed plenty of time for the wind to dry out the potatoes and change the sugars to starch. With advice from the potato experts, Kroc created his own natural curing process with a big electric fan. And bingo! The fries now tasted just like those in the original restaurant, and the same process could be replicated in all new stores.[9]

Kroc also describes how he developed a *proprietary system* that would deliver consistency for both customers and franchisees:

- Consistent menu — no variants allowed — and the same methods to attain the same food quality.[10]
- Sparkling clean toilets, restaurants, and parking lots. *Cleanliness* was one of the four principles that Kroc stressed, along with *quality, service*, and *value*.[11]
- No pay telephones, jukeboxes, or vending machines of any kind.
- Founding the "Hamburger University" for franchisee and staff training.

- Offering franchisees a simple product by providing them with a suitable ready site and financing.
- Keeping the economics favorable, with a narrow product line, and helping the best suppliers to serve a large number of McDonald's outlets and lower their costs, for example through bulk packaging and allowing them to deliver more items per stop.[12]

Any business person writing their memoirs will — like Ford and Kroc — make the most of the opportunity to advertise the quality of their product. Yet it is clear that Kroc, Ford, and Kamprad all realized that the main purpose of their systems was to deliver a good product at an exceptionally low price. The bigger the scale of the operation, while allowing no variation in product and procedure, the lower the price. And the lower the price, the greater the customer satisfaction, sales, profits, and value of the company. Kroc kept the price of McDonald's hamburgers at fifteen cents for nineteen years — until 1967, when inflation brought about by President Johnson's Great Society and the Vietnam War forced an increase. He authorized the increase to eighteen cents reluctantly: "If you look at it from the customer's point of view — which is how I do it, because this guy is our real boss — you see the importance of every penny."[13] This is the credo of every price-simplifier.

Who created the greater value — the McDonald brothers or Ray Kroc? It depends on your perspective. Financially, Kroc added far more. Yet, we could argue that the brothers created the product, the proposition, the brand, the pricing, and indeed the system. The changes to their template since 1961 have been relatively minor. However, imitation is usually more vital than creation. Certainly, in this case, imitation created an extraordinarily valuable business with a global footprint. Ray Kroc added a simple, uniform, high-quality franchise system that cloned the McDonald's formula to a degree that was truly mind-boggling.

Results

- McDonald's was the first restaurant to create an assembly-line operation that recreated the coffee shop with a limited but complete meal solution. The firm also first made the fast-food restaurant a universal phenomenon. It created a new branch of the restaurant business, a template for fast-food specialists in chicken, pizzas, and innumerable other food genres, which in aggregate have dwarfed even McDonald's.
- By the end of 1976, McDonald's had 4,177 restaurants. Seven years later, this had nearly doubled to just short of 8,000. Ray Kroc died in 1984, still in harness. Today, the firm serves 68 million customers every day in 35,000 restaurants and 119 countries, from Panama to Russia to New Zealand.
- In 1976 the revenues of the McDonald's Corporation (excluding the sales of franchisees and affiliates, including only their payments to McDonald's) exceeded $1 billion and net earnings after taxes were over $100 million. In 2014 revenues were $28.1 billion, and net income was $8.8 billion. The firm is worth $93.5 billion today — 39,000 times what the McDonald brothers received when they sold out to Ray Kroc in 1961. This compares with a meager twenty-fivefold increase in the

Standard & Poor's index over the same time period. Kroc (and his successors) therefore added some $90 billion of value to McDonald's by spreading the formula that Dick and Mac McDonald had invented but could not — or would not — propagate.

Key Points

1. McDonald's is another example of price-simplifying — where subtraction and an assembly-line operation have slashed complexity and enabled costs to be halved. Could you automate an industry or service that has not yet experienced anything comparable?
2. If you work in a service business, take heart that price-simplifying works as well in a service or retail setting as it does in manufacturing.
3. With prices cut in half and the appropriate economic exploitation, world demand for fast-food hamburger meals has expanded to a degree that was unimaginable in 1948. Can you think of a pedestrian market today that could conceivably explode in a similar fashion if prices were at least halved through automation and co-opting customers and/or franchisees?
4. Once again, the simplifying firm created a new, proprietary business system, with economics quite different from those of more complex restaurants. If you are considering price-simplifying, how might you create a dramatically better economic system than whatever exists today in your market?
5. The firm combined an exceptionally low price with greater usefulness (consistently high-quality food; play

areas for children), art (especially the Golden Arches and instantly recognizable branding) and ease of use (speed). What might be the equivalent extra benefits in your industry?

6. The McDonald's formula was invented in miniature by its two founders. It was made into an economic powerhouse by one person who took the system, standardized it, and cloned it on a scale that its creators could never imagine. So look for a simplifying system that already exists on a tiny scale but could be made into a universal product and rolled out around the globe.

Victory Over Big Brother
The Real Story of 1984

*He made devices simpler by eliminating
buttons, software simpler by eliminating
features, and interfaces simpler by
eliminating options. He attributed his love
of simplicity to his Zen training.*

Walter Isaacson

This is the story of a man and a machine that transformed
the way we work and play. He distorted and compressed
reality, and achieved the impossible by insisting on simplicity and its benefits for customers.

There had been nothing like it before. In the middle of
Super Bowl XVIII, immediately after a touchdown, came
images conjured up by Ridley Scott, the director of *Blade*

Runner. Masses of skinheads in an urban wasteland are paying full attention to Big Brother on a huge screen. But then a female athlete wearing a white top labelled "Macintosh" leaps clear of pursuing police to hurl a sledgehammer that smashes the screen and destroys Big Brother. "On January 24th," announces the voice-over, "Apple Computer will introduce the Macintosh. And you'll see why 1984 won't be like *1984.*"

The sixty-second commercial cost $750,000 to make and $800,000 to air. But it was well worth it. All three of the main U.S. networks featured stories about the advertisement that night, and the publicity it generated was huge. *Advertising Age* and *TV Guide* both later voted it the greatest commercial of all time.

"Big Brother" was a thinly veiled reference to IBM, commonly called "Big Blue." In October 1983, *Business Week* had opined that the battle for market supremacy in personal computers "is already over. In a stunning blitz, IBM has taken more than 26 percent of the market in two years, and is expected to account for half the world market in 1985. An additional 25 percent of the market will be ... IBM-compatible machines."[1]

At the public launch of the Macintosh on January 24, 1984, Steve Jobs, chairman of Apple, attacked IBM directly. After detailing the crimes, follies, and misfortunes of the much larger company, he built towards his climax: "It is now 1984. It appears that IBM wants it all ... and is aiming its guns at its last obstacle to industry control, Apple. Will Big Blue dominate the entire computer industry? The entire information age? Was George Orwell right?"[2] Jobs had the crowd of journalists and commentators hollering and cheering. Then came a rescreening of the commercial, which generated a standing ovation. It was a dramatic launch for what turned out to be a rather special machine.

The build-up to 1984 had started in the early 1970s, when computer technology began to change and a wave of simplification began, as the microprocessor made computing faster, cheaper, and easier to operate. In 1975, the MITS Altair became the first mass-produced personal computer kit, but it was much less sophisticated — as well as much cheaper — than the many microcomputers that were emerging at the time. For $495, the hobbyist got a pile of parts to solder to a board; even assembled, it was pretty primitive.[3]

One of those hobbyists was Steve Wozniak; another was his friend, Steve Jobs. In 1975 they began working on the Apple I, a step up from the Altair, but still an unprepossessing machine. The Apple II, a much neater product, quickly followed. The first real packaged computer, it came in a sleek and friendly plastic case modelled on the Cuisinart food processor; and it could be plugged in and used straight out of the box. Its simplicity made the computer a general consumer product for the first time: you didn't need to be a geek to use it.[4]

Jobs' biographer, Walter Isaacson, says Jobs "liked the notion of simple and clean modernism produced for the masses … he repeatedly emphasized that Apple's products would be clean and simple." In Jobs' own words, "We will make them bright and pure and honest about being high-tech … that's our approach. Very simple … the way we're running the company, the product design, the advertising, it all comes down to this: Let's make it simple. Really simple."[5]

Yet the real breakthrough came not with the Apple II but with the work being done at the Xerox PARC research labs at Palo Alto. Jobs secured an invite for himself and his team at the end of 1979 and he was amazed by what he saw. Up to that time, all computers had used command lines that required some operator skill, and there were no user-friendly graphics. But the Xerox engineers had invented the "desktop" — a screen that could have several documents and folders on it at the same time, represented by icons. A device they called a mouse was used to access the one you wanted with a simple click. When he saw this demonstrated, Jobs was captivated. "THIS ... IS ... IT!" he exclaimed. "It was like a veil being lifted from my eyes. I could see what the future of computing was destined to be."[6]

All of these features were included in the Xerox Star. Launched in 1981, it was the first recognizably modern PC. But the Xerox Star retailed at $16,595, and only 30,000 of them were ever sold. If it was to trigger a revolution, the Xerox Star needed to be simplified.[7]

The Apple Lisa, introduced in January 1983, was the first computer on which users could drag a file across the desktop, drop it into a folder, scroll smoothly through a document, and overlap a series of windows. Through Jobs' famous WYSIWYG — What You See Is What You Get — the Lisa also enabled users to print off *exactly* what they saw on the screen. The Lisa 2, introduced a year later, cost $3,495 — about a fifth of the price of a Xerox Star for a greatly superior machine.[8] The Macintosh was a further advance — it cost $2,495 and had many charming features that made it both easy and fun to use, including a superb graphics package and a great variety of different fonts, documents, spreadsheets, and other templates.

In truth, the first Mac was far from perfect. Its gorgeous

user interface required far more memory than it possessed. Over time, however, the necessary improvements were made, and, as we'll see later, the appeal of the Mac to a certain type of user — broadly creative types and those who revel in good design — made it a huge long-term commercial success.

But Jobs was not a price-simplifier. One of his early co-conspirators on the Mac project — and the man who named the machine — was Jef Raskin, a young, brilliant, and highly opinionated computer scientist. Raskin wanted to build a computer for the masses, to go into every home — a utopian and preposterous idea, it seemed, at a time when fewer than one in a hundred homes owned computers. His ideal was a machine with a keyboard, a screen, and the computer itself in one unit, priced at $1,000. If Jobs had supported this notion, Apple might have become the Ford Motor Corporation of computers. He could have done so, which would have made him a price-simplifier. But he had a different idea, as Walter Isaacson explains:

"Jobs was enthralled by Raskin's vision, but not by his willingness to make compromises to keep down the cost. At one point in the fall of 1979 Jobs told him to focus on building what he repeatedly called an 'insanely great' product. 'Don't worry about price, just specify the computer's abilities,' Jobs told him. Raskin responded with a sarcastic memo."[9]

A power struggle ensued. Jobs prevailed; Raskin left the company. In 1984, the Mac was priced at a 25 percent premium to the rival IBM PC, an inferior machine in everyone's eyes, except for the majority of buyers.

Jobs was not obsessed with price or with the creation of a mass market for his machine. He simplified principally to make his PC *better* for the user. He made a device that he himself wanted to use. He was not wholly uncommercial: he simplified so that his machines were easier to produce and therefore cheaper; and he introduced some stunning cost savings relative to the Xerox Star. But he reduced cost and price *only* when doing so did not compromise his main objective, which was to make a fabulous computer. Ease of use, art, and usefulness made his machine a joy to use. Price was important too, but markedly less so. Ever since, no Apple device has been sold *primarily* on price.

Therefore, Jobs is the first of our second breed of simplifier — those we call *proposition-simplifiers* — because the overwhelming innovation and advantage lie in the proposition of the product or service, not in its price. In Jobs' own phrase, the product has to be "insanely great." In our phrase, the product must be a *joy to use*; it must have a palpable "wow factor." Jobs spoke for all the proposition-simplifiers we will meet in this book when he said, "products are everything."[10]

By relating the stories of Ford, IKEA, and McDonald's, we showed that the overwhelming benefit brought to customers by price-simplifiers is a massive price reduction of anything between 50 and 90 percent. This reduction is absolutely essential for price-simplifiers. We then showed that Ford, Kamprad, and the McDonald brothers attempted, where possible, to improve the ease of use, usefulness, and aesthetic appeal (art) of their products, provided this did not conflict at all with the overwhelming aim of a low — and continually lower — price.

With proposition-simplifiers, the position is exactly

reversed. Their absolute priority is to make the product or service not just a little better, but a whole order of magnitude better, so that it is recognizably different from anything else on the market. The Macintosh, the iPod, the iPad, and the Apple watch all met this criterion: the proposition was either a great improvement on an existing product or else a totally new, unique creation. It had to be insanely great, a joy to use. At least one of the dimensions we specified as optional extras for price-simplifiers — ease of use, usefulness or art — *must* be present in a proposition-simplifier's new product or service. In fact, usually two or three of these benefits must be present; but whether it is one, two or all three of these advantages, they must transform the proposition.

In the case of the Macintosh, all three benefits were evident, with ease of use the most important:

1. Ease of use:

   - Simple to set up and plug in.
   - Escape from the DOS command mentality that was still used in all other machines at the time. Even the path-breaking IBM PC, launched in 1981, used old-fashioned command-line prompts to drive the operating system.
   - The Macintosh operating system, with its desktop and bitmapped graphical displays, was far more intuitive and required less training and expertise than the DOS systems.

2. Usefulness:

   - The ability to store and access documents on the desktop.

- Overlapping windows that scrolled perfectly.
- The ability to compose a document and print it exactly as it appeared on the screen.

3. Art:

- Playful and intuitive icons.
- Wide range of beautiful fonts.
- The hardware design was clean and light — an attractive consumer product in comparison with IBM's gun-metal grey.

These features were the *raison d'être* of the Macintosh. Price reduction was a subsidiary, much less important objective. In fact, as we shall see later in the book, most proposition-simplified products and services — such as the Mac — sell at a premium to their rivals.

In designing the Lisa and the Mac, Jobs' reference point was the Xerox Star. He was interested in dramatic cost reduction, but only if it coincided with product improvement. For example, the mouse. The Xerox mouse had three buttons and didn't roll smoothly. Also, because of its many features, it cost $300. So Jobs commissioned a design house to come up with a $15 mouse with one button and smooth rolling even on a rough surface. Before long, they had developed one.

Jobs' main purpose was not to re-engineer the Xerox technology to make it commercially viable. He wanted to surpass it — to enable users to move a window around the desktop, drop it into a folder, increase or reduce its size, all simply by manipulating the icon, with no need to select a command before doing so. The Xerox Star couldn't do any of this. The Mac could do all of it, and more.

Which Type of Simplifying is Better?

It depends:

- on what the entrepreneur or executive wants to do,
- on what his or her firm is able to do,
- on the opposition,
- on the market,
- on the technology, and
- on the time and place.

Neither approach is inherently superior to the other.

The big advantage with price-simplifying is that it is often possible to build a huge mass market *and* a business system that cannot be imitated and out-scaled easily — at least not after the early days — which effectively shuts out all rivals. The price-simplifier is likely to end up with much higher volume than the proposition-simplifier, for the latter relies on the customer's willingness to pay a premium for a demonstrably superior product. The rub for proposition-simplifiers is that they need to keep ahead of their rivals through constant innovation and new product development — otherwise, they will lose market share and suffer falling margins. Yet they may be able to build an extremely valuable, loyal following, and brand among the middle to top of any given market. The price-simplifier must price down the experience curve, passing on cost savings and keeping margins tightly constrained. In contrast, the proposition-simplifier can — *sometimes* — hang on to fat net margins: up to 40 percent in the case of Apple, which at the time of writing was the most valuable company in the world.

The history of computing shows that there can be room for *both* a price-simplifier and one or more proposition-simplifiers to weave their magic within the same broad market. But any company that tries to pursue an approach that is halfway between the two is destined to fail. The Mac never reached double figures in terms of overall market share, so it never slayed the mighty IBM. What helped IBM and IBM-compatible machines was that Microsoft eventually duplicated most of the features of the Mac's operating system. Windows 1.0 was not launched until the autumn of 1985, and it was initially a poor imitation of the Mac's (and even the Xerox's) operating system. But gradually the gap was closed, especially between 1985 and 1996, when Jobs was exiled from Apple and there was little reinvestment in Macintosh software.

Even so, the laws of simplicity saw to it that IBM was not the main beneficiary of its Faustian pact with Microsoft. IBM continued to be outflanked in terms of product quality by the Mac, and then lost most of its remaining market share to price-simplifiers — initially Compaq and Hewlett-Packard, and later Dell. As a company, IBM was always a reluctant simplifier, pursuing neither proposition-simplifying nor price-simplifying with any great vigour. Over the life of its involvement with PCs, it never made any money from them, bleeding cash to such an extent that the whole firm nearly collapsed. In 2005 Big Blue made its last computer and sold the husk of the business to a Chinese rival, Lenovo.

And what of plucky little Apple? Its share of the computer market fell to just 3 percent during the barren Jobs-less years, but it did just fine after the Second Coming of Steve in 1997. Jobs rationalized the product line, developed new software with impressive wow appeal and, together with the firm's new design supremo Jony Ive, triumphed with the iMac, launched in 1998 as a desktop computer for the home market. Priced at $1,299, the iMac sold 800,000 units in its first five months, the highest run rate that Apple had ever had.[11] During the 2000s, the Mac reached new heights when it became the hub for other Apple devices. It took more than two decades, but proposition-simplifying finally paid off in spades. As with Henry Ford's price-simplifying, Steve Jobs didn't reach the summit in a single bound. Self-belief and doggedness eventually proved just as essential as the right strategy.

Results

- On the stock market in May 2000, Microsoft was worth twenty times more than Apple. Ten years later, Apple overtook Microsoft, and a year later it was worth 70 percent more than its chief rival.[12] As we write, Apple is worth $742 billion.

- In 2010, Macintosh's global market share in computers was just 7 percent, yet it accounted for 35 percent of the industry's operating profits,[13] higher than any other company. Apple created and dominated the top segment of the PC market and was rewarded with very attractive returns.

- Without Apple, it is unlikely that computers today would be so elegant and easy to use. Without Apple, the desktop we all take for granted today might not have become the common currency of computers.

Key Points

1. Steve Jobs was a different kind of simplifier from our previous examples. He was a *proposition*-simplifier who aimed to make an "insanely great" product. Do you find it easier to imagine yourself as a *price*- or a *proposition*-simplifier? What about your company?

2. Price-simplifiers create or enlarge a mass market. With the Mac, Apple served the middle and upper echelons of users, who were willing to pay a significant premium for a more intuitive, useful, and beautiful product. Do you think this might work in your industry?

3. In the same broad market, price- and proposition-simplifiers can happily coexist, each with their distinctive customer appeal, and each with their distinctive commercial advantage. For price-simplifiers, it is a mass market. For most proposition-simplifiers, it is higher net margins. Which of these advantages do you think your organization would value more?

4. The worst fate, as with IBM, is to fall between the two simplifying stools — to be out-proposition-simplified and out-price-simplified. No matter how iconic the brand, how lofty the reputation, how high the installed base of users, how clever the executives, or even how rich the company, for those stuck in the middle, the knacker's yard beckons. Is this a danger for your firm?

5

The Strategy Simplifiers

Strategy should be a punch between the eyes.

Bruce D. Henderson

The strategy simplifiers transformed the business world. Not only did they spawn a huge and highly profitable consulting industry, they also allowed young people to learn about business more quickly than ever before, and thus lowered the average age of chief executives. They also reinvented business theory and grounded it securely in economics, and in financial and marketing theory. Business became less intuitive and more analytical, a process that has now been overdone, but at the time made it possible to use resources much more effectively.

When I (Richard) was finishing my MBA at the Wharton Business School in 1975, I attended an interview with the

Boston Consulting Group, then a small management consultancy firm, and asked what was different about their practice. "Basically, we have a model which guides our consulting," my interviewer, Philip Hulme, said. He went on to explain the Boston Box, with its cash cows, dogs, question marks, and stars. I was instantly gripped by both the clarity of his answer and the prospect that huge businesses could be guided by something so simple, and helped by someone like me, a green twenty-five-year-old. So when BCG offered me the job, I immediately accepted.

I soon came to understand the scale of the transformation implied not just by the model but by the whole premise of BCG's existence. Before Bruce Henderson set up the firm in 1963, top-level boardroom consulting was dominated by the venerable firm of McKinsey, and the archetypal consultant was a grizzled veteran who had seen and done it all and was now offering advice to the industry in which he — it was always a he — was an acknowledged expert. In effect, McKinsey sold experience.

BCG, by contrast, sold distilled intellect. Its typical consultant was an MBA whose youth and brains either frightened or bemused clients. But whereas McKinsey tended to use individual consultants or small teams, BCG supplied a simple, universal model that was applicable to any business or industry. There had never been such a model before; nor has there been a simpler one since, and certainly not one that contains so much truth. BCG said it was better to be a market leader than a follower, and that firms should "price down the experience curve" — that is, gain market share in order to reduce costs and prices and therefore attain a lower cost position than any competitor. The best position was a "star business": that is, a market leader in a high-growth market. Such positions were inordinately valuable. BCG claimed that over the lifetime of a product, nearly all the cash made by any company would be derived from businesses that were or had been stars.

This advice, incidentally, largely coincides with the price-simplifier strategy, minus this book's emphasis on simplifying as the *means* to become a star and create a huge market.

BCG's model greatly simplified the advice for any large firm. It told the corporate center *and* operating managers what to do — focus on their stars, increase market share everywhere, cut costs, and pass the benefits on to customers through ever-lower prices.

I saw first-hand how useful this advice could be. There were some dangers and errors in the theory, but overall it worked, saving companies from making expensive mistakes and pushing them in the right direction. The belief in a simple model and the intellectual force behind it also had a galvanizing and uniting effect on firms that bought into the BCG model. It supplied a common language and logic, shared from the boardroom down through divisions and operating units. The belief that radical improvements were possible in market share, profit and the value of the firm was energizing, reinforcing the economic logic at the core of the advice. Belief in ideas — broadly the right ideas — created huge wealth.

BCG simplified and both the company itself and its clients prospered.

This was pure proposition-simplifying. BCG made no attempt to cut prices: generally, it followed the rather high hourly rates of the market leader, McKinsey. This was a sensible strategy, because the market for high-quality consulting is not price sensitive. Chief executives and boards want the *best* advice, and they are willing to pay for it. A cut-price offer would merely have called the firm's credibility into question.

So what was BCG's appeal?

1. Ease of use:

- Previously, business strategy was either not considered at all, or was considered too complex to reduce to a simple model. But now it was possible to determine the position of any business and what to do with it by knowing two simple pieces of information: its market share relative to its largest rival; and the future market growth rate. The position within the Boston Box could be estimated in real time, and checked later. The chart could be used by the boardroom or by managers in a small business unit. It told everyone what to do. Business strategy suddenly became demystified — it was now accessible and even fun; and it could be communicated hundreds of times more concisely, effectively and memorably than before.
- The simplicity of the ideas made them easy to grasp and turn into action.

2. Usefulness:

- The advice was useful because it was based on simple and powerful micro-economic concepts. Market share was useful because it lowered costs. Having higher market share than competitors, and therefore lower costs, enabled prices to be reduced and market share to be increased yet further. Competitors would make lower returns and become less interested in the market. If prices were kept sufficiently low, rivals might even be forced to exit the market altogether, increasing the leader's market share.

- BCG's system required client executives to think for themselves, based on BCG's ideas, rather than merely follow expert advice. Internalization of the ideas created the ability and commitment to implement them, and to adapt the strategy when circumstances changed.

3. Art:

- The Boston Box lent itself to colorful, attractive, and simple visual presentations that made the concepts come alive and applicable to client circumstances.
- The elegance and simplicity of BCG's concepts were explained in "Perspectives" — short, well-written tracts — and at CEO conferences held in luxury hotels.

BCG simplified not only the consulting "product" but the process. Because they were simple, the consultancy's ideas were easily taught to new consultants. And because the consulting was based on ideas, those consultants did not need to have decades of experience. The new consultants were relatively cheap, so simplicity also lowered the cost of production, as it usually does. As a result BCG grew faster than McKinsey and became more profitable because it charged similar fees but incurred lower costs.

There is a certain irony here, because BCG's business

SIMPLIFY

model — the one it used for its own commercial and strategic decisions — was different from the one it preached. In
our terms, BCG assumed that every business should be a
price-simplifier. That is broadly correct. Most markets are
like that. But BCG — and many other firms — can operate
successfully within the proposition-simplifying model.[1]

Another terrific proposition-simplifier — in the same field
but with a different proposition — was Bain & Company, a
firm that split off from BCG in 1973 amid some acrimony. I
left BCG to join Bain in 1980 and was amazed how different
the two firms were, despite adhering to the same concepts.
In those days, Bain's proposition was extremely innovative,
daring, and simple. It simplified its client base. It simplified
its objective. And consequently it simplified the process of
consulting.

Bain was different from all other consulting firms in the
world because it only ever worked for the group CEO of a
company. Right from the start, even when it was a tiny firm,
this gave Bain elite status. Its sole objective was to increase
the market value of its client companies, and thus grow itself.
Results would follow from the right strategy — which Bain
promised to work out — but only if that strategy were implemented wholeheartedly. Only the top dog had the power to
make that happen, so Bain refused to talk to anyone else.

The proposition to the chief was invariably simple and
audacious. We (Bain) will put the technology we possess —
the vast power of strategy (remember, this was the 1970s and
1980s) — exclusively at your disposal. We will never work for
any of your competitors. We will advance your interests —
both yours personally and those of your firm — since, with
our advice, you will be following the right strategy and you

will be the right pilot. So you can trust us with all your secrets.

But (Bain would continue) we require something from you in return. You must agree never to work with any of *our* competitors (BCG, McKinsey, and so on). You must also take our recommendations seriously. Of course, since our proposals will be based on data and logic, you can challenge the data and the logic. But unless you can prove us to be wrong, you must follow our suggestions. Moreover, no arbitrary limit may be set on the Bain budget. If we deliver continued increases in profit and market value — and you get a good return on the money you spend with us — you should follow our recommendations for the next steps, including our budget.

Bain assumed all responsibility for explaining the strategy down the line. Indeed, before any new strategy and recommendations reached the CEO and the board, Bain outlined everything to everyone — from the lowest to the highest managers — correcting any mistakes and securing consensus along the way. This process of securing consensus for its recommendations flushed out any disagreement from powerful "barons' within the management structure — for example, the head of a division or a region. Since the rules of the Bain process dictated that data and analysis were paramount, it was hard for any baron to disagree, even though his or her intuition or personal interests might dictate otherwise. Meanwhile, the CEO's power vis-à-vis the next level down was greatly increased, which made his or her life much simpler and easier.

The path envisaged was one of ever-closer symbiosis between Bain & Company and the client . . . and ever-higher consulting revenues. Participating in this virtuous cycle — and perhaps getting very rich by doing so — was heaven.

I should add, however, that Bain & Company's proposition has since changed, to my nostalgic regret. Its product line and practice have become much more extensive and variegated as the boardroom consulting market has exploded into a huge number of micro-segments. Both Bain and BCG have become more like McKinsey — less providers of "pure" strategy and more hypermarkets of specialized experts, returning the compliment McKinsey paid to BCG in the 1970s when it entered the strategy market in a big way.

The original Bain & Company strategy was simple because it cut through and across all the corporate politics within a firm. The interests of the firm's CEO and Bain were totally aligned, elevating the power of both. For the CEO, it was a joy to employ Bain for several reasons:

1. Ease of use:

   - Life for the CEO became hugely simpler. He now had first-class strategic insight with which to dazzle the board, he knew what to do, he had a trusted confidant and sounding board completely outside the organization's tentacles, and he had all the data and analysis he could possibly need to persuade everyone of what he wanted to do. He could also be confident that, barring unforeseen disasters, his tenure was going to be very successful and his options worth a fortune.

   - The power of the CEO and his or her ability to force through radical change were greatly enhanced.

2. Usefulness:

- Bain was enormously effective in raising the market value of its clients.
- Its process generated huge energy among managers and channeled it in a single direction. One senior manager described the Bain consultants working in the bowels of his organization as "like nuclear reactors generating wave upon wave of commitment and excitement."

3. Art:

- The spiel from Bain's partners to the CEOs was original, slick, and effective — basically because it was true. The art lay especially in the originality — the CEOs had never heard anything like it before.

During the 1970s and 1980s, Bain grew much faster than BCG, overtook its alma mater, and became very profitable. Today, it has over 6000 employees, compared with BCG's 9700. They are now two of the three most prestigious consulting firms in the world (with the third being McKinsey).

The difference between BCG and Bain may seem esoteric to anyone who has not dealt with a "strategy consultant." Yet I was staggered by the differences in the way the two firms behaved, despite using the same intellectual material for their work. These were two very different business systems, sold differently, which selected and wooed their clients differently, with a different *modus operandi* both within the consulting firms themselves and in their interactions with clients. Since then, whenever I have been able to observe two competitors in the same field, I have been sensitive to the subtle differences that can lead them to play the game in disparate ways. This is to the advantage of both firms, because it blunts the edge of competition between them. If the differences are very large, as they are between BCG and Bain, they do not compete head-to-head, and each firm can have a dominant share of "its" market segment.

This is how it is with proposition-simplifying — it is possible for two firms, such as BCG and Bain, each to develop a unique proposition. Moreover, the success of a previous proposition-simplifier does not stop a new firm from developing a new proposition, which may — indeed *should* — appeal to a different set of customers, newly defined by the proposition-simplifier with their fresh formula. The possibility of multiple proposition-simplifiers in what is apparently a single market is in marked contrast to what happens with price-simplifying, where, as the biggest part of the market must be served, there are typically fewer degrees of freedom in configuring the business. For example, if you want to make cars cheaply to compete with Ford, you need a huge factory and a moving assembly line, just like Ford's. If you want to sell furniture cheaply, you need to commission relatively few suppliers to make it, transport it in flat packs and stock it in huge, out-of-town stores. In other words, your business system must be identical to IKEA's. The quest for the lowest-cost universal product and business system tends to result in a similar answer every time. Since the target is most of the market, there is less basis for segmentation or differentiation. Any firm trying to find the lowest-price solution will probably have to create a similar product and system.

So when a price-simplifier creates a mass market, it tends to collapse segmentation within the existing market, or at least decimate the sales of other players in that market. There is just one new mass market, offering the lowest price and the greatest value. Other segments may decay or die. McDonald's invents the hamburger restaurant, that market grows exponentially, and mom-and-pop coffee shops and greasy spoon cafés hit hard times. Budget airlines create a mass market, and full-service airlines lose market share. It is the same with IKEA or any other price-simplifier. They suck out at least some of the oxygen previously enjoyed by traditional competitors because price is a singularly potent weapon that becomes even more powerful over time. Scale advantages compound as the business system of the leader expands internationally, the cost advantage gap between the leader and other competitors widens, as does the price gap, making it virtually impossible for the followers to catch up. The leader, if the business is run well, should become ever more dominant over time. This is why so many of our price-simplifying case studies have been successful for decades.

But the pattern is different with proposition-simplifiers. Instead of reducing or collapsing the degree of difference between competitors, the difference and distance between them may increase. New market segments may be layered on to an existing market, sometimes with minimal damage caused to established firms. BCG did not really damage McKinsey; in fact, it created a new market for the old dominant firm (the strategy consulting market). Similarly, Bain's success did not spell the downfall of BCG. Where price is not a key purchase criterion, where value for money is hard to compare between rivals, and where new ventures may find ways to delight new, specialized groups of customers (as with Bain, which exclusively served the chief executives of large companies), the arrival of new proposition-simplifiers may enlarge the market and its profitability, meaning that there is plenty of room for several successful players, rather than just one.

But not always. When a proposition-simplifier comes up with a clearly superior formula — one that appeals to a large part of the previous mainstream market — the effect may be to crush most of the traditional competitors. Uber is a case in point, as are smartphones. Although the new generation of mobile phones is much more expensive than their predecessors, they are so much more appealing, convenient, and useful — with enticing new apps added all the time — that they have already transformed the market. As a consequence, Nokia — which was slow to develop a smartphone — has suffered greatly at the hands of Apple and Samsung.

Insofar as we can generalize, the two forces that do most damage to previous segmentation — those that tend to collapse segmentation in a market, rather than create independent new segments and leave old ones largely intact — appear to be *price* and *technology*. And when these converge in a free service that utilizes a novel technology — such as Google — the effect on the traditional market (in this case, print media) can be utterly devastating.

Results

- In 1963, McKinsey enjoyed a virtual monopoly in boardroom consulting for top companies. In the early 1970s BCG became a credible competitor in this lucrative market, and Bain & Company joined that gravy train in the late 1970s. Since then, despite the emergence of high-quality "boutique" rivals, these three firms have remained the most prestigious consultancies, with each establishing itself as a global brand.

- The market for boardroom and strategy consulting — with the latter being a large subset of the former — has grown enormously since 1963. The best estimate is that the worldwide market has grown by around 16 percent each year since then, which means it is now more than 2000 times bigger. McKinsey had revenues of $7.8 billion in 2013 and employed 17,000 people. The following year, BCG reported revenues of $4.6 billion and had a total staff of 9700. Bain & Company does not publish its revenues, but it employs 5400 people. (Pro-rating its revenues by staff, compared to BCG, gives an estimated revenue of $2.6 billion.) These are stunning numbers for three firms that were members of little more than a cottage industry back in the 1970s. All three are also astonishingly profitable, with returns on sales varying between about 15 and 40 percent. Moreover, all of the expansion has happened organically, without any need for external capital.

Key Points

1. Proposition-simplifying is often a great opportunity for service businesses. If simplifying can increase usefulness, ease of use and art, revenues can be multiplied at the same time as margins expand.
2. The proposition's value can usually be greatly increased by simplifying. All it requires is sufficient imagination

and empathy — an ability to put yourself in the shoes of the least price-sensitive and most profitable customers.

3. Whereas there can be only one successful *price*-simplifier in any given market, there can be more than one *proposition*-simplifier, each with a differentiated proposition. Can you think of a proposition that will allow you to carve out a new market and provide your new target customers with a service that greatly increases ease of use, usefulness, and aesthetic appeal to them?

4. Now it's time to become up to date with three very recent examples of simplifying that have used the internet and the smartphone as the platform to provide new or sensationally improved services.

6

Taxi! The Brave New World of Apps

If it ain't broke, break it.

Richard Pascale

Something interesting is happening. Uber, the world's largest taxi company, owns no vehicles. Facebook, the world's most popular media owner, creates no content. Alibaba, the most valuable retailer, has no inventory. And Airbnb, the world's largest accommodation provider, owns no real estate.

Tom Godwin

In this chapter, we look at three further instances of proposition-simplifying, all of which now seem so obvious that we wonder why they didn't happen years earlier.

Proposition-simplifying can make life easier and more pleasant, and can make a fortune for the simplifier. Perhaps the value of simplifying and how to do it are only just starting to be fully understood. Perhaps, also, the internet and associated technologies are making it easier to simplify and transform a market almost overnight.

Uber and Easy Taxi

If you live in Paris, or one of many other big cities, getting a cab can be a nightmare. The strict regulation system in the French capital means that drivers have to pay hundreds of thousands of euros for their "medallion," which means that the rides are expensive, especially as the number of cabs is kept deliberately below the level of demand. Consequently, it is often impossible to hail a cab in the late evening or at weekends, or when it's raining hard. Moreover, drivers often have to stop to ask directions, and you never know how much the fare will be or whether you will be taken to your destination via the scenic route.

However, since 2009, this age-old system, and similar variants throughout the world, has started to crumble and die. In you live in a big American city, or increasingly elsewhere — from London to Singapore to Bangalore — you will already probably be well aware of the brave new world of Uber. You install a smartphone app, enter your credit card details, and the next time you need a cab, you open the app and enter your pick-up location and destination. You will be told how long the cab will take to arrive, and two minutes before the driver reaches your location you will receive a text message. The cab is usually cleaner and smarter than a traditional taxi. The driver always knows where he or she is going because the car has built-in GPS. When you arrive at your destination, your card is charged automatically and you are emailed a receipt, so there's no need to carry cash. You can share the fare with friends if you like, in which case the bill is divided between the members of the group. No tip is necessary. After the trip, you can rate the driver; and you may well have checked out previous ratings before your ride. If you give a driver only three stars you may receive a follow-up call from someone in customer services wanting to know what went wrong. You have security and peace of mind, because every driver is known and every car is tracked. Uber encourages civility, so you are told the driver's name and he or she knows yours.

Uber works well for the drivers, too. They rate the service's clients. The time and energy they would otherwise spend cruising the streets for fares is eliminated and their uptime is increased. Several drivers have credited Uber with improving their potential earnings substantially.

Fares may be cheaper than in a normal taxi, depending on location, but the big advantage of Uber is the proposition, not the price. It provides all three of our three customer benefits from simplicity:

1. Ease of use:

   - Simplifies the ordering process — no hailing, no phoning, no searching.
   - Reduces uncertainty of when the car will arrive and the type of vehicle.
   - Simplifies the payment process — the system is entirely cashless.

- No need to tip — indeed, it is not even possible (except with cash payments).
- Makes it easy to split the fare.
- Makes the price transparent with an accurate fare estimate for your trip.

2. Usefulness:

- Security and peace of mind through tracking.
- Better quality through rating driver and passenger on every trip.
- Universality — a single app works in most major cities around the world.
- Saves time through seamless on-demand dependability.
- Automatic electronic receipts.
- Choice of services, from everyday to luxury cars.

3. Art:

- The experience is a revelation when compared with traditional taxis.

In sum, it is a joy to ride in an Uber cab.

The system itself is extremely simple, not least for the company itself. It owns no cars. It is just an intermediary that uses technology to connect riders with drivers, then takes a slice of each transaction.

Uber was founded in San Francisco in 2009 by CEO Travis Kalanick and Garrett Camp. They devised the software app that enables the system to work, recruited drivers in San Francisco, and launched the site in 2010. Since then, Uber has spread to 250 cities throughout the world, constrained only by legal and regulatory challenges as traditional taxi drivers fight a rear-guard action, and a handful of imitators who got in first in a few cities, notably London. Although the regulatory issues are serious, the new way of catching a cab seems set to kill traditional taxi firms stone dead.

Uber has been incredibly successful already. Although it was started with very little money, on 15 May 2014 the *Financial Times* reported that Uber had raised $1 billion of funding at a $10 billion valuation.[1] Seven months later, the firm raised a further $1.2 billion, but now the reported valuation was more than four times higher — $41 billion.[2] And in May 2015 the company was reported to be raising a further $1.5–2 billion. By then, the valuation had increased to $50 billion[3], and in November 2015 is said to be up to $70 billion[4].

As impressive as these valuations are, Uber's operational growth is even more staggering, and the main reason why it has been able to raise such colossal funding. At the time of writing it was estimated that Uber would be operating at an annualized rate of $10 billion of ride value by the end of 2015,[5] from which it will earn approximately $2 billion in commission. Two billion dollars of net revenue for a six-year-old company is simply extraordinary.

Uber is the most outstanding recent example of proposition-simplifying, so it warrants close inspection. Of course, the company echoes several of the characteristics of other proposition-simplifiers, but it also reveals much about how proposition-simplifying can work today.

One of the more remarkable aspects of Uber has been how the company was able to grow in its early days. In September 2011 one of its blog posts reported:

"Uber spends virtually zero dollars on marketing, spreading almost exclusively via word of mouth. I'm talking old school word of mouth, you know at the water cooler in the office, at a restaurant when you're paying the bill, at a party with friends — 'Who's Ubering home?' 95 percent of all our riders have heard about Uber from other Uber riders. Our virality is almost unprecedented. For every seven rides we do, our users' big mouths generate a new rider. Imagine if twitter got a new user every seven tweets?"[6]

The speed at which a truly compelling proposition can diffuse through word of mouth in a superconnected world can be surprising, and another reason why analysts and onlookers habitually underestimate the growth and potential size of simplifiers.

But word of mouth is only one aspect of Uber's growth potential. Other figures imply that the company is not only capturing market share but increasing the size of that market. Travis Kalanick stated in early 2015 that the traditional taxi market in San Francisco is about $140 million per year, while Uber's gross revenues in that city are now approximately $500 million per year — a good three times larger than the traditional market. Moreover, Uber's revenues in San Francisco are tripling each year and should continue to grow for several years yet, which will easily make it ten times larger than the whole of the old market.

Even this understates Uber's growth potential, though. The company is already going beyond merely being a taxi service. It is experimenting vigorously, and may become a much broader logistics service, spanning personal on-demand transport, ride pooling, personal logistics, such as deliveries and transporting kids to school, car replacement, and even business logistics. It certainly has the potential to steal market share *and* increase market size in many of these areas.

At this point, after so many accolades, one might conclude that Uber was always going to be unbeatable once it perfected its service. After all, it created a disruptive experience that radically simplified the taxi proposition; it had a very direct revenue model that earned a handsome cut of every transaction; customers seemed happy to do the heavy lifting of attracting other customers, so there was no need to spend fortunes on marketing and advertising; and, as we have seen in San Francisco, it could build a multi-million-dollar business in just one city, even before it expanded into hundreds of others.

So, we might ask, why did Uber need to raise all those billions of dollars? Why couldn't it fund its growth through its own surging cash flow? Wasn't the original proposition-simplifying idea good enough to ensure success?

The answer is that success was certainly not assured, and it was probably a near-existential decision to raise the amount of funding that the company did in 2014–15. There were fundamental characteristics of Uber's service, and how it had to operate within its markets, with which the company's leaders had to grapple. In particular, they faced three dramatic threats.

First, Uber's basic service is easily and cheaply replicable. By way of comparison, imagine what you would have to do to build and supply a viable rival to a single IKEA store. That would be far more difficult and expensive than gathering together a few good software developers to build an app and a support system, organizing a few hundred drivers, and marketing your new taxi service. Unsurprisingly, then, very few companies have attempted to copy IKEA, whereas Uber has been copied hundreds of times in various countries around the world, in many cases with less than a million dollars of investment capital. The importance of this cannot be overstated. For Uber to succeed over the long term, it has had to grow at a phenomenal rate in order to shut out its rivals. And that exponential growth rate is becoming even more crucial, since some of those rivals are now receiving heavy backing and have global ambitions.

A case in point is Easy Taxi, the Samwer brothers' clone of Uber, which operates in thirty countries, mostly in Latin America, the Middle East, Africa, and Asia. With $77 million raised at the time of writing, it is not even the best funded of Uber's competitors, but it is notable because of who is behind it.

Oliver, Alexander and Marc Samwer — founders of Rocket Internet in Germany — have practically turned cloning good ideas into an art form, scouring the United States for proof of concept, then rolling the idea out in dozens of countries simultaneously. Few startups are able to transition to a multi-country rollout, create the required management infrastructure, or attract the investor base to fund such ambitious expansion plans in the tight timeframes within which Rocket Internet operates. The Samwers leave product and proposition formulation, as well as proofing the concept in the market place, to other entrepreneurs, then muscle in to appropriate and spread the idea. They specialize in just one skill — building and rolling out the business system as rapidly and efficiently as possible in any attractive open market they identify.

While this strategy might offend our creative sensibilities, it is brutally effective. Rocket Internet when public in October 2014 with a valuation of 6.7 billion. The brochure listed sixty-one companies in which it has invested, eleven of which have been "proven winners." To those who criticize his lack of innovation, Oliver Samwer says: "In the internet business there are Einsteins, and Bob the Builders. I'm a Bob the Builder."[7]

The second threat faced by Uber is that its rivals not only poach valuable customers but also degrade Uber's service characteristics while improving their own. Imagine pick-up times in a city with five rival taxi firms, each of which operates two hundred cars. Now imagine the same city has one operator with six hundred cars, while the other four firms have only one hundred each. In the latter case, the large operator will consistently deliver far shorter waiting times than any of the smaller operators. Its ability to optimize the efficiency of its pick-up and delivery network creates a much better service. This is a very powerful network effect — being largest matters, and it is very dangerous to be substantially smaller than the market leader. Such markets invariably consolidate down to one or two main competitors over time, as the leading firm's product or service becomes far better than the rest simply because it is bigger.

Finally, Uber had to address the fact that its business is initially local, city-by-city. To realize the advantages of a better-optimized pick-up and delivery network and not suffer the disadvantages of being a follower, the company had to launch in hundreds of cities around the world at the same time in order to pre-empt competition. This rapid rollout gave the firm another advantage, too: because Uber established a presence in so many cities, its business customers soon began to realize the benefits of using a single app wherever they were in the world. Hence, the competitive footprint and success conditions for competitors started to become harder than merely achieving dominance in a particular city.

So, far from assuming success is guaranteed, Uber has had to behave like a fearsome and paranoid competitor. In August 2014 the *Wall Street Journal* focused on Lyft, a smaller San Francisco-based competitor of Uber, and declared: "Forget Apple versus Google. The fiercest battle in the tech capital may well be between two heavily financed upstarts plotting the demise of the taxi industry — and each other."[8] Uber has rapidly adjusted its service offering to check Lyft's advance. The former was initially a white-glove town car service, but it moved rapidly to offer a more mass-market service based on mid-range cars in response to Lyft's launch positioning. Tales of sharp competitive practice have been rife. Lyft has accused Uber of poaching its drivers in order to disrupt its network growth; and both companies have accused the other of ordering and cancelling cars to interfere with service levels. Uber's stance against regulators and unclear legislation has been equally aggressive: get in first; conciliate the regulators later. And, after relying on word-of-mouth marketing in its early days, Uber is now pouring money into recruiting drivers and advertising its services everywhere.

And as we have seen, Uber has been a prodigious fundraiser and a fierce competitor. The management and execution challenges multiply when you decide to build in 250 cities across five continents and fight a dozen well-backed regional competitors all at once. In these circumstances the ability to raise plenty of cash becomes a critical competitive weapon. This will probably continue for quite some time. Since Uber has proven the previously unimagined scale of the revenue opportunity in proposition-simplifying sectors of transportation and logistics it has started to see a very different kind of animal enter the arena. In February 2015, for instance, Bloomberg reported: "Google is developing its own Uber competitor — the two competitors are going to war over self-driving taxis."[9] Google is reported to be testing its ride-sharing app with its own employees, attracted by the relevance to its long-running initiative on self-driving cars, and no doubt intrigued by the "fire hose of data about transportation patterns within cities." Life in this space seems set to remain fascinating for the foreseeable future.

As with the wheel, the steam engine or the semiconductor, some technological advances are widely applicable to many problems and markets, and they trigger an explosion of further simplifying across a range of activities. The internet and its mobile extension through the smartphone are surely two of the most powerful simplifying platform technologies today as they can create global access to billions of customers. We now look at two more powerful simplifiers that have been facilitated by these recent developments.

Spotify

A few years ago, you were probably still fumbling around with CDs (and their cracked cases), feeling very modern by paying iTunes 99p for every song you wanted to hear on your first-generation iPod, or being very naughty and downloading tracks for free from a shadowy peer-to-peer file-sharing service that never paid the artists a penny. It would have been an outrageous idea to think that you might have access to most of the music in the world. Now, though, sixty million people can make that claim, courtesy of Spotify: three-quarters of them use the service for free and put up with annoying adverts between the music, while the other quarter pay £9.99 per month for an unfettered, all-you-can-hear experience. The latter group are also able to save playlists to listen to offline.

Spotify is another profound consumer proposition-simplifier, and it displays some of the familiar characteristics. Judging from our own experiences with the service, it almost certainly increases our consumption of music, and perhaps how much we are prepared to pay for music over a lifetime, even though it is completely free for most of its users. It has also grown in a highly viral way, just like the early Uber, because the proposition is so strong and even more social — users share their playlists with friends and can follow other users' playlists and favorite artists.

In two respects, however, Spotify is radically different from Uber. First, it was extremely hard to develop the service and then launch it. But second, having cleared those initial hurdles, Spotify became global almost effortlessly.

The value chain that Uber attacked was weak, fragmented, poorly organized, and largely indefensible. Spotify, by contrast, had to co-opt the concentrated, legally fortified, and calcified grip that four major record labels had on the entire music industry. Because this was so difficult to execute, requiring enormous upfront investment, and because it was not something that could be imitated with a million dollars and a few talented developers, the Spotify story developed in a very different way from Uber's. When you look at Spotify's competitive environment, there are many competitors, but very few of them are serious (Apple Music being a notable exception) or able to attract major funding.

The difficulty of imitation seems to have given Spotify, which now boasts over twenty million licensed tracks, a wide lead over any rival. It is not just about discovery, as in the case of competitors such as Pandora. On Spotify, users can listen to any artist or any song they want. Its largest rival is the French company Deezer, which operates in 180 countries (Spotify is in only 58), but Deezer has only sixteen million users, with only six million of them paying customers.

Airbnb

Like the taxi industry, in the 2000s the hotel sector was ripe for disruption. In many cities, hotels in central locations were (and still are) overpriced and lacked the "atmospheric" character of the place itself. Airbnb enables homeowners to offer their couches, spare rooms or entire homes for rent for short stays, and the company has become a network of over 25,000 active hosts in 190 countries. More than twenty million guests have booked thirty million nights on the platform since it was founded in 2008.

The beauty of the proposition lies in the experience. For the host, it is now easy to operate a "hotel," however modest, with global reach of potential guests. Meanwhile, the guests can request anything from a room in a shared apartment with a local host to a country estate or a villa by the sea. This is obviously a more local experience than staying in a characterless hotel, advertised with the slogan "belong any-where." The experience is also easy. You search for a city, list the number of guests and number of nights, and ask for a room in a shared home (with the host) or an entire home (without the host). Then you are able to specify a particular neighborhood, host language or amenities. Finally you scroll through the matched listings and reviews.

Many guests make their bookings entirely on the basis of the reviews. When you arrive, you meet the host, receive the keys and get advice about the property itself as well as what to do in the neighborhood. After your stay, you are encouraged to review the host and the property, and your payment is transferred.

Airbnb enables hosts to supplement their income from an asset they already own. The company has done a tremendous job of ensuring quality profiles of properties and giving the owners an efficient system to manage all aspects of the transaction — from booking, property profiles, and guest verification to payment and insurance.

Like Uber, Airbnb has come under pressure from the industry it is disrupting. The legality of generating revenue from renting out private property has raised alarm bells from regulators, particularly in cities such as New York, where vested interests have formed anti-Airbnb groups and launched hostile ad campaigns. In response, the company has now started to work with city authorities in order to ensure its operations are fully legal. Some rival companies have also appeared, although all of them are far less success-ful, with far lower profiles, than Airbnb.

Airbnb has already raised $800 million and the company is valued at $20 billion. It now offers more lodging options than any hotel chain in the world. And, like Uber, its advantages over its traditional rivals are obvious:

- For both guests and hosts, it's easy to find and list properties.
- It's easy to filter properties based on availability.
- The payment process is simple.
- It's universal — you can book in 190 countries.
- By clicking one button, a host can schedule a photographer to present their property in the best light.
- The guest's ID can be easily verified.
- Both guests and hosts have access to — and can write — detailed reviews.
- Hosts can get insurance easily.

Back to Uber: Results

- Uber has the highest valuation of any private company currently backed by venture capital, and this has been achieved in just six years. The company raised more than $3 billion from a wide range of blue-chip venture capitalists in twelve months.
- In January 2015 Uber had approximately 160,000 active drivers operating in the United States alone. Figures suggest that unless their after-tax costs average more than six dollars per hour (petrol, depreciation and insurance), the net hourly earnings of these drivers exceed the hourly wages of employed taxi drivers and chauffeurs.[10]
- The early evidence suggests that Uber can multiply the size of the taxi market, perhaps by ten times or more, in many of the 250 cities where it operates.

Key Points

1. As with price-simplifying, proposition-simplifying can dramatically enlarge a market. While price can make a product affordable for more people, a better proposition can result in much more frequent use of a product.

2. If you are a strong proposition-simplifier, you can create word-of-mouth referral, resulting in explosive growth with little investment in customer acquisition. If you move first and/or fastest, you can gain an enormous advantage in building the best service — because of the iron laws of networks — as well as really strong barriers against your rivals. One further important advantage of moving fast is that it enables you to raise substantial funding on the most attractive terms: that is, at the highest valuations. Speed therefore reinforces a virtuous circle.

3. Where it is relatively easy to imitate a product or service, constructing a business system around it which builds barriers against your opponents becomes vital for your long-term success. In Uber's case the ability to use the service in every U.S. city, and in most of the world's other major cities, confers a huge edge.

4. Network effects, economies of scale and other volume-based economic "goods" necessitate an intensified competitive stance. If you are playing in one of these markets you have to become the leading firm, and you have to do it *really* fast. So, if you can, destroy or marginalize your rivals in the early days.

5. The "economic goods" do not change over time, and the same is generally true of the elements of business

systems. But platform technologies change constantly. New enabling technologies are often leading indicators of where the next great wave of innovation can be created.

We'll shortly invite you to consider whether you and your firm should become a price-simplifier or a proposition-simplifier. But first we need to consider the nature of these two strategies a little more, as well as the trade-offs that each must make to generate an earthquake in the market.

7

The Two Strategies and Their Trade-offs

I wouldn't give a fig for the simplicity this side of complexity; I would give my right arm for the simplicity on the far side of complexity.

Oliver Wendell Holmes

The two simplifying strategies are very different — in what you have to do to make them happen, in what your objectives are, and in the way you are rewarded for success. By comparing and contrasting them, we can begin to think about which you and your firm might be able to execute before anyone else has the same idea. But the two strategies also have something in common. At their heart is the imaginative use of trade-offs, baked into a unique business system, to outfox competitors and deliver a product that the target market will buy in droves.

We've seen that there are two "natural positions" to transform a market:

- Price-simplifying: Create a *mass* market — simplify to make a product or service dramatically *cheaper*. Simplicity results in the product being easier to make, so simplicity for the *producer* matters most. The producer operates on low margins but enjoys massive growth in revenues.
- Proposition-simplifying: Create a *premium* market — simplify to make the product or service dramatically *better* and *a joy to use*. Simplicity results in the product or service being easier to use and usually more useful and/or aesthetically appealing, so simplicity for the *user* matters most. The producer enjoys high margins and growth in both revenues and profits. The premium part of the market will normally be a smaller part of the total market than with price-simplifying, although in some cases proposition-simplifying can create a *new* mass market, as with smartphones.

We can illustrate the two strategies as shown in Figure 1.

In either case, the market is greatly enlarged, but the mass market will normally end up being several times larger than the premium market. On the other hand, the margins from the premium market may be several times greater, so the absolute profit opportunity and the return on cash invested may be high and broadly similar whichever strategy is adopted. The only exception is the bonanza that may accrue if proposition-simplifying also generates

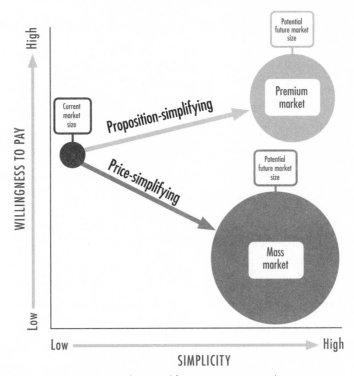

Figure 1: The simplifying opportunity chart

a mass market, as with some of Apple's devices, but this phenomenon is rare.

At this stage, all we are seeking is a rough, visceral sense of whether you and your firm may adopt either strategy; and if so, which one. The market size and returns are necessary but insufficient bases for you to decide to pursue either strategy. (As we will see in the next chapter, other very important factors must be considered, too.) Yet, somewhere along the line, one of the two simplifying strategies will need to spark your excitement. Picture what major success might look like, then decide between them.

Three Precepts for the Price-Simplifier

1. Use simplicity to make something *much cheaper* both to make and to supply. This must always be the primary objective.

2. In making the product cheaper, *simplify to eliminate* what we call "expensive utility" — anything the customer can do without. Henry Ford eliminated variety of car models, features and, eventually, colors. The McDonald brothers dispensed with waitresses and broad menu options. Ingvar Kamprad provided one style of furniture, reduced variety within each product category, and eliminated certain transport costs through self-assembly.

3. *Increase utility* where it can be provided at little or no extra cost. Substitute *cheap* utility for *expensive* utility. Henry Ford provided a lighter, more robust car that was easier to drive and maintain, but did so at no extra cost through simple design, lighter materials, and an automated production system. Dick and Mac McDonald provided better hamburgers and fries than were available at the local coffee shop, but because they sold so many of them — and automated production — they were able to charge only half the price. IKEA sells furniture that is not only inexpensive but well designed, while also providing play areas and crèches, inexpensive restaurants and sometimes entertainment for the kids — real benefits that pay for themselves by attracting a larger flow of customers.

Deciding which elements of utility to remove and which to substitute requires imagination, and putting yourself in the shoes of the mass-market customer. Think about each of our three categories separately:

- Greater *ease of use*. What could this mean in your market?
- Greater practical *usefulness* of the product or service. How could you provide this?
- Greater *art* — everything that makes a product or service attractive, yet cannot be reduced to hard usefulness or ease of use. Is this a dimension that is missing in existing products or services?

Two Precepts for the Proposition-Simplifier

1. The primary objective is to use simplicity to make something *a joy to use* — to add utility through greater ease of use in the first place; then greater usefulness and/or art.

   In the epigraph at the start of this chapter, we quoted U.S. Supreme Court judge Oliver Wendell Holmes: "I wouldn't give a fig for the simplicity this side of complexity; I would give my right arm for the simplicity on the far side of complexity." In other words, you may have to work through greater complexity in order to provide greater simplicity to your customers.

   The Macintosh illustrates this perfectly. The great thing about the Mac when it emerged in 1984 was that it provided an accessible, modern PC — the desktop made life so much easier for the user, when compared with the old type of personal computer where you had to write code to get it to do anything. The ability to access files in a flash by clicking on an icon, to print a page exactly as it appeared on the screen, and to scroll smoothly through a document were huge break-throughs in terms of ease of use, utility, and art. But what was easy for the user was not easy for Apple to provide. In fact, writing the Mac's software was horren-dously complex. Apple's engineers went through hell to reach the simplicity on the far side of complexity. And it took chief rival Microsoft another two or three years to develop a barely acceptable Windows version.

More than half of the battle is knowing what the end result should be. To get there, you either have to make a huge leap in imagining what would make life simpler for the customer — in effect, what the experts at Xerox PARC had achieved as early as 1979 — or, like Steve Jobs, see an early prototype and realize where it is head-ing and how it might be improved. The end result for the proposition-simplifier is always a giant vault forwards in terms of simplicity and utility for the customer.

2. A secondary objective is to use simplicity to make the product cheaper to make; or at least to ensure that the extra utility far outweighs the extra cost.

Making Clever Trade-Offs

When developing new products and business systems, designers always have to make trade-offs — that is, they have to decide between two positive attributes, since they can't have both together to a great degree. For example, car designers have to trade off power for fuel efficiency, or vice versa — you can't have fast acceleration and power *and* high mileage per gallon. Another common trade-off is that of high service against low price — as, for example, with a taxi versus a bus. The art is to make trade-offs that appeal to a particular customer segment and give them what they *really* want to a higher degree than any other product. Make trade-offs that benefit both your firm and your customers.

For the price-simplifier, this is straightforward. The central objective is always to reach a very low price — which the customer will value enormously — by trading off attributes that your customers think are less important. Imagine a haggling conversation with a typical customer. For instance, the person who invented the supermarket might have said to his target customer, "If you are willing to push a trolley around my big shop, pick the products you want yourself, and take them to the till, I will charge you much lower prices than your local grocery store." Similarly, imagine the McDonald brothers saying, "If you will line up for your meal and accept a limited menu, we will cut the price of your burgers in half." Or Ingvar Kamprad: "If you will drive some distance to my giant warehouse of a store, follow the signs, and go the long way round so you have to walk past dozens of products you weren't intending to buy, pick your furniture, push it to the checkout, drive it home, and assemble it yourself, I will give you stylish goods at prices you won't believe."

Yet it's usually not enough to slash prices without providing some other benefits, too. Even Aldi offers the convenience of a large parking lot and enticing "job lot" merchandise in addition to rock-bottom prices. Cunning price-simplifiers always substitute cheap benefits for the expensive ones they eliminate. The latter may include staff. There is an implicit deal with the customer: "Put your back into some of the heavy lifting that is done by our rivals' employees, and you will get a fantastic price and plenty of other benefits, too."

At IKEA, you get good design, entertainment to keep your children amused, and a wide range of products to take home immediately. At McDonald's, you get great prices, high-quality burgers and fries, fast and efficient service, cheerful surroundings, kids' play areas, and spotlessly clean toilets. Amazon offers unbeatable prices — which is hardly surprising when you consider its scale and wafer-thin margins — but also a one-click service, extensive product reviews, and super-fast delivery.

The principle is slightly less obvious, but equally true, for proposition-simplifiers. They make deals with their more affluent customers, with the latter persuaded to pay a *little* more for something that they believe is *much* better. The way to square this circle is to go through the complex process of simplifying what is bought. Think of the examples already mentioned: the speed and intuitive nature of a Macintosh; the ease of use and peace of mind in taking an Uber cab; the insight and rapid results for a chief executive who seeks advice from BCG or Bain & Company.

But the highest form of making a trade-off comes when the trade-off is not really a trade-off at all — what we call a "virtuous trade-off."

Virtuous Trade-Offs

Instead of choosing between two good things, if you are very lucky or very creative, you may be able to trade off something bad against something that is good.

At the start of the Second World War, it was evident that there was going to be a shortage of steel and other metals among all the combatants. But Britain had a plentiful supply of wood . . . and furniture-makers. So Geoffrey de Havilland designed a very simple but fast bomber that could be made almost entirely out of wood, and flown by just two men. The raw material made the plane lighter than its rivals, enabling it to be fitted with smaller and simpler engines. It was also easier and cheaper to build. By using wood and eliminating protective armor and defensive gun turrets, de Havilland enabled his "Mosquito" to fly at well over four hundred miles an hour, making it faster than any German fighter and therefore impervious to air attack. Manpower and operating costs were halved, and fatalities almost eliminated. De Havilland pushed through his simple design in the teeth of Air Ministry opposition: the establishment could not believe that a bomber without protective guns and armor plating was a viable proposition.

The genius of the Mosquito was that it transcended the traditional trade-off between weight and speed. The more protection a plane possessed (a good thing), the less speed it could achieve (a bad thing). Protection versus speed had always seemed an inescapable dilemma, but the Mosquito changed all that. Since no enemy plane could catch it, it needed no armor plating. So it could be even lighter. Suddenly there was no trade-off — the speed *provided* the protection. With the Mosquito, pilots had both unbeatable speed and unparalleled protection — the two went together, creating a virtuous circle. It was as if de Havilland had suddenly discovered how to give a Ferrari the fuel economy of a Mini.

The plane proved to be an immense success. In 1943 the Commander in Chief of the Luftwaffe, Hermann Göring, admitted, "It makes me furious when I see the Mosquito. I turn yellow and green with envy."[1]

Virtuous trade-offs are different from normal hard-choice trade-offs. If you can make a virtuous trade-off, you end up with *two* good attributes, instead of one good and one bad. This is really creative simplifying — ingenuity that trumps iron laws. Many "giving back" attributes of price-simplified products are really virtuous trade-offs in disguise. For instance, if a private art gallery offers visitors a nice big glass of champagne when they walk through the door, knowing that its sales and profits will increase as a result, it is deploying a virtuous trade-off — between giving away glasses of champagne and profits. Similarly, IKEA's free entertainment and play areas boost revenues and profits. The trade-off is virtuous. The stuff for kids is a genuine benefit, but its cost is illusory. Both customers and the company win.

A Visit to London Zoo

In 1935 the publisher Allen Lane, who was waiting for a train at Exeter station, was unable to find a good, inexpensive book at the bookstall to read on his long journey back to London. This started him thinking, leading him to the conclusion that he should price-simplify.

Lane wanted the quality of a hardback combined with the low price of a paperback. At the time, paperbacks were generally reprints of old titles, usually by dead authors, and they were shoddily produced to cut costs. Hardbacks, by contrast, were so expensive that they were beyond the pockets of most working people. Lane thought that if he could push the price down to sixpence (around £1.50 or $2.25 in today's money — a figure that even Kindle books rarely match today), he could create a new mass market by tempting ordinary people to buy books rather than borrow them from public libraries. The main problem was that it was expensive to buy the rights to high-quality, contemporary fiction. Substituting a paper cover for a hard one would save some money, but nowhere enough to reduce the price by the necessary 90 percent. Lane's next step was to persuade everyone — authors, publishers assigning rights, bookstores, and his own company (Penguin) itself — to accept lower margins. The authors' initial recalcitrance was voiced by George Orwell: "In my capacity as reader I applaud the Penguin Books; in my capacity as writer I pronounce them anathema."[2] Lane then cut his costs further by moving the company out of its expensive central London premises and onto a large site in Harmondsworth in what was then rural Middlesex (it now overlooks Heathrow Airport). He was charged £2000 for the land and £200 for the cabbages growing on it. But still the sums didn't add up.

Lane needed a new approach and finally he spotted one that had eluded both himself and everyone else. His great idea was to sell Penguin books from non-traditional outlets — in particular kiosks, such as the one in Exeter station that couldn't offer him a decent cheap read, and general stores. The first breakthrough came when Woolworth's, the top mass-market general store, agreed to take 100,000 Penguins on consignment. Almost immediately, Lane's titles were available in far more outlets than other publishers' books, so he was able to order much larger print runs and thereby reduce unit cost. Initial runs for popular hardbacks were around five thousand at the time, while for Penguins they could be twenty thousand. That meant the goal of sixpence per book was achievable, since production costs were now so much lower. Lane narrowed his list down to just ten titles, then sold the entire list to his outlets, rather than the individual titles.

Allen Lane invented a whole new publishing business system — a mass market based on distribution that was much wider than anything that had been attempted before. The principal advantage for customers was that prices were roughly a tenth of those for comparable hardbacks, yet the quality was still high. The roster of authors was first rate, too. Lane's first ten titles were all written by bestselling novelists at the top of their game, including Agatha Christie, Ernest Hemingway, André Maurois, Compton Mackenzie, Beverley Nichols, and Mary Webb. The uniform design was arresting: the book title, in a white band, was framed by two borders of color — orange for novels and green for crime — with the famous Penguin logo — drawn by a nineteen-year-old office junior during a visit to London Zoo — centered below. The design became a classic, and an updated version of the logo is still used today. In contrast to the prevailing cheap paperbacks, Lane used decent paper and bindings that were made to last for years. Penguin's wide distribution network also made the books easier to buy at times when they were most desired by potential readers.

At the heart of the Penguin revolution, though, was a virtuous trade-off. Lane avoided the traditional trade-off between price and quality by redefining quality in terms of the *contents* of the book, not the cover's material. He recognized that, as we would say today, books are software, not hardware. His simple system — based on a limited list, a new distribution channel and high print runs — made it possible to produce high-quality books at extremely low prices.

Note, though, that at the root of the virtuous trade-off lay an enormous expansion of demand. The depth of Lane's insight — or gamble — can be gauged by contrasting the contemporary and well-argued view of George Orwell that Penguin Books would lead to a *decline* in the amount of money spent on books:

"The Penguin books are splendid value for sixpence, so splendid that if the other publishers had any sense they would combine against them and suppress them. It is a great mistake, of course, to imagine that cheap books are good for the book trade. If you have, for instance, five shillings to spend [about £15 or £22.50 in today's money], and the normal price of a book is half-a-crown [£7.50 or £11.25 today] you are quite likely to spend your whole five shillings on two books. But if the books are sixpence each, you are not going to buy ten of them, because you don't want as many as ten; your saturation-point will have been reached long before that. Probably you will buy three sixpenny books and spend the rest of your five shillings on seats at the 'movies.' Hence the cheaper the books become, the less money is spent on books."[3]

The great flaw in Orwell's argument was that he considered only *prosperous* book-buyers, those who had five shillings — the weekly wage of a laborer — to spend on books or some other pastime. Laborers could afford no more than sixpence for a book, but they wanted to own books just as much as their rich neighbors did. So once Lane was able to cut his cover price to that extraordinarily low level a huge number of working- and lower-middle-class people suddenly became book-buyers for the first time in their lives.

So it goes. A price that is a fraction of the previous price for a desirable item will always create a vast new market. Moreover, the size of that market is always greatly underestimated, even by sage observers such as George Orwell. Therein lies the marvelous opportunity for price-simplifiers.

Conventional thinking will never lead you to a virtuous trade-off. You have to be willing to construct a new route to virtue via lateral thinking or a novel argument. For instance, "If we do X, then we should arrive at a virtuous trade-off. We can avoid a trade-off that everyone else thinks is inevitable, such as one between a well-produced popular book and a high cover price."

In your market, can you find a way to increase an important *consumer* benefit while also increasing your own *supplier* benefit? Can you see a connection between any one of the benefits in the left-hand column and any one on the right? (Look beyond the benefits that lie next to each other.)

Consumer Benefit	Supplier Benefit
Power or performance up	Market share and volumes up
Easier to buy	Costs down
Easier to use	Profits up
Speed of consumption	Speed of delivery
Advantage of being in a larger network	Advantage of being in a larger network
Lower prices	Lower costs
Higher standards	Greater customer loyalty and retention
Greater consistency	Lower cost of recruiting customers

Self-service benefits customer	Self-service benefits supplier
Lighter	
More portable	
New segment of consumers	

Key Points from Part One

1. There are two reliable strategies for successful simplifying to create a very attractive star business that can stand the test of time. However, the two strategies you may use are very different. Price-simplifying focuses on "simple to make," relying on a spectacularly low price to generate a mass market. Proposition-simplifying makes the product a joy to use — easier, more useful and more aesthetically pleasing. It is time for you to consider whether either strategy could be successful in your market, and whether it could be devised and executed by you and/or your firm.

2. Price-simplifiers substitute cheap customer utility for expensive customer utility.

3. Proposition-simplifiers work through the complexity of a sophisticated product or service until it becomes really easy to use.

4. Both types of simplifier must be adept at making trade-offs — delivering superb value for money yet also high profits. This is achieved through shrewd and original redesign of the product and how it is delivered. How might you do this in your market?

5. The ideal is to transcend normal trade-offs by discovering "virtuous trade-offs" — where you have two good attributes rather than one good and one bad attribute.

New virtuous trade-offs are always out there, waiting to be unearthed. The best of them are great for the customer, great for the firm and lethal to competitors. What might be your virtuous trade-off?

Conclusion

We hope we have given enough examples to convince you that there are two attractive and viable ways to create a valuable new star business through simplifying. If you are convinced and enthusiastic, you need to decide which of the two strategies will fit your market opportunity, your skills and those of your firm, and be the most difficult for your competitors to adopt or replicate. Once you have chosen your strategy, flesh it out in detail and work out how to execute it brilliantly. You need to think profoundly about the economics of your market and of your existing and prospective competitors. You must also consider what will be required to sustain simplifying success.

In brief, you will need to learn *how* to simplify for your own market.

No plan, it has been said, survives contact with the enemy. That's true enough. But the more deeply you think before you act — and the more you know about what has caused other simplifiers to win or lose — the better your project launch will be, the more prepared for what lies ahead you will be, the more adroit your improvisation will be, and the greater your chance of magnificent success will be.

Part Two is our best attempt to gird your loins for the fight.

PART TWO

How to Simplify

In Part Two, we map out in detail *how* to simplify by describing what you will need to do for each of the two strategies. As in Part One, we proceed by mixing examples of what successful (and sometimes unsuccessful) simplifiers have done in the past with lessons and rules of thumb that we have distilled from our case studies and from the most useful principles of strategy.

There is more texture in this part, and our first case, Honda, is an instructive vignette of how a wholly inappropriate strategy can be corrected by "contact with the enemy" — that is, by encountering inconvenient market reality and rival firms. With the benefit of historical hindsight, we hope you may gain a degree of prefabricated foresight, or at least be alert to the pitfalls and how to surmount the roadblocks you will inevitably meet along the way.

For reasons that will become apparent, in this part we reverse the order of Part One, dealing with how to proposition-simplify before tackling how to price-simplify.

But before we get to the "how," we must first address the

issue of "which." Price- and proposition-simplifying are both game-changing strategies, but they are mutually exclusive. Which is the right one for you? The next chapter will help you decide.

8

Which Type of Simplifier Will You Be?

Modern industry never looks upon the existing form of process as final. The technical basis of that industry is therefore revolutionary.[1]

Karl Marx

To be a price-simplifier or a proposition-simplifier — that is the issue.

Here are four questions that will help you decide which one you should be:

1. Do your firm's *attitudes* — its policies and culture — make it more disposed to pursue price-simplifying or proposition-simplifying?

2. Has a *competitor* already occupied one or both of the target positions?
3. Can you *see the key* to unlocking either position?
4. Does your firm have people with the necessary *skills* to execute the target strategy? If not, do you know how you might recruit them and from where?

For an interactive version of this test, visit www. SIMPLIFYforCEOs.com, which will help you select which of the two simplifying strategies better fits your organization.

The Attitude Test

Try taking the test that is presented over the next few pages. Give your first response without thinking about it for too long. Your answer should be placed on the scale from 0 to 10 that appears below each question. Place a tick on the scale to indicate where your firm currently resides. In most cases, the answer to the question will be either a straight "Yes" or "No"; so, wherever possible, choose either 0 or 10. Move towards the middle of the scale only when there is no clear answer. Note that "Yes" is sometimes positioned on the left of the scale, and sometimes on the right (and the same is true for "No," of course). You may add your ticks to the book itself so you have a permanent record of your answers, or — if you want to keep the book pristine — you could always photocopy the pages of the test.

1. Do you believe that your firm or a competitor could cut costs and prices by more than 50 percent?

   a. No

   b. Yes

NO (a)   YES (b)

☐ ☐ ☐ ☐ ☐ ☐ ☐ ☐ ☐ ☐ ☐

0   1   2   3   4   5   6   7   8   9   10

2. If you started again from scratch, would you see more potential in:

   a. Making the product or service a joy to use

   b. Making it simpler so that you could cut prices by a large amount

(a)   (b)

☐ ☐ ☐ ☐ ☐ ☐ ☐ ☐ ☐ ☐ ☐

0   1   2   3   4   5   6   7   8   9   10

3. What are the operating margins in your business? (Operating margin is EBIT — earnings before interest and tax — divided by revenue.)

   a. Over 25%

   b. 11–25%

   c. 10% or less (including losses)

(a)   (b)   (c)

☐ ☐ ☐ ☐ ☐ ☐ ☐ ☐ ☐ ☐ ☐

0   1   2   3   4   5   6   7   8   9   10

4. Are you currently the lowest-cost and price competitor in your market?

   a. No

   b. Yes

   (a)   (b)

   □ □ □ □ □ □ □ □ □ □ □

   0   1   2   3   4   5   6   7   8   9   10

5. Has your firm invested in state-of-the-art systems to speed product or service flows and drive out cost?

   a. No

   b. Yes

   (a)   (b)

   □ □ □ □ □ □ □ □ □ □ □

   0   1   2   3   4   5   6   7   8   9   10

6. Which do you think is more important — your firm's operating margin or the return on cash invested?

   a. Operating margin

   b. Return on cash invested

   (a)   (b)

   □ □ □ □ □ □ □ □ □ □ □

   0   1   2   3   4   5   6   7   8   9   10

7. How long is your time horizon when you make a serious capital investment?

   a. 1–5 years

   b. 6–10 years

   c. More than 10 years

   (a)   (b)   (c)

   □ □ □ □ □ □ □ □ □ □ □

   0   1   2   3   4   5   6   7   8   9   10

8. How important is revenue growth to your firm?

    a. Important

    b. Vital

    (a)   (b)

    ☐ ☐ ☐ ☐ ☐ ☐ ☐ ☐ ☐ ☐ ☐
    0 1 2 3 4 5 6 7 8 9 10

9. Is — or was — the founder of your firm:

    a. A visionary obsessed with "insanely great" products or services, making them a joy to use and solving customer problems

    b. Frugal and penny-pinching

    (a)   (b)

    ☐ ☐ ☐ ☐ ☐ ☐ ☐ ☐ ☐ ☐ ☐
    0 1 2 3 4 5 6 7 8 9 10

10. Is your firm's culture:

    a. Meritocratic/elitist — the top 5 percent of the firm make or break it

    b. Egalitarian — for example, similar office space and facilities for everyone, emphasis on teamwork, no reserved parking spot

    (a)   (b)

    ☐ ☐ ☐ ☐ ☐ ☐ ☐ ☐ ☐ ☐ ☐
    0 1 2 3 4 5 6 7 8 9 10

11. Does your firm believe in using simplicity mainly:

    a. To make products/services better

    b. To make products/services cheaper

    (a)   (b)

    ☐ ☐ ☐ ☐ ☐ ☐ ☐ ☐ ☐ ☐ ☐
    0 1 2 3 4 5 6 7 8 9 10

12. Is it important for your firm to hide complexity from customers so that the product/service is easy for them to use?

a. Yes

b. No

(a)   (b)

☐ ☐ ☐ ☐ ☐ ☐ ☐ ☐ ☐ ☐ ☐
0   1   2   3   4   5   6   7   8   9   10

13. Is the product/service's usefulness, ease of use, and appearance or emotional appeal to customers very important to the firm?

a. Yes

b. No

(a)   (b)

☐ ☐ ☐ ☐ ☐ ☐ ☐ ☐ ☐ ☐ ☐
0   1   2   3   4   5   6   7   8   9   10

14. Is the price of the product or service the most important thing?

a. No

b. Yes

(a)   (b)

☐ ☐ ☐ ☐ ☐ ☐ ☐ ☐ ☐ ☐ ☐
0   1   2   3   4   5   6   7   8   9   10

15. Does the firm believe that being the leader in the market overall or being the leader in a premium segment that will pay more for the product is more important?

    a. Being the leader in the premium segment

    b. Being the leader in the market overall

(a)   (b)

☐	☐	☐	☐	☐	☐	☐	☐	☐	☐	☐
0	1	2	3	4	5	6	7	8	9	10

16. Which do you think is more important — investment in people or investment in production and delivery systems for customers?

    a. Investment in people

    b. Investment in systems to deliver consistency for customers and to keep costs low

(a)   (b)

☐	☐	☐	☐	☐	☐	☐	☐	☐	☐	☐
0	1	2	3	4	5	6	7	8	9	10

17. How important is constant and relentless innovation in your firm?

    a. Vital

    b. It's more important to get the business system right to start with, and then make gradual improvements afterwards

(a)   (b)

☐	☐	☐	☐	☐	☐	☐	☐	☐	☐	☐
0	1	2	3	4	5	6	7	8	9	10

18. Which is more important in your firm?

a. Developing new projects

b. Making the existing business system run smoothly

(a)   (b)

☐ ☐ ☐ ☐ ☐ ☐ ☐ ☐ ☐ ☐ ☐

0   1   2   3   4   5   6   7   8   9   10

19. Is there a continual buzz about change in your firm, or is it more valuable to do the basics right every time?

a. Buzz about change

b. Basics right every time

(a)   (b)

☐ ☐ ☐ ☐ ☐ ☐ ☐ ☐ ☐ ☐ ☐

0   1   2   3   4   5   6   7   8   9   10

20. Which is the better description of your firm?

a. Dynamic and free-wheeling

b. Disciplined and predictable

(a)   (b)

☐ ☐ ☐ ☐ ☐ ☐ ☐ ☐ ☐ ☐ ☐

0   1   2   3   4   5   6   7   8   9   10

21. How much does your firm encourage risk-taking?

a. It is fine to take big risks, even if they don't pay off

b. Only moderate risk-taking is acceptable

(a)   (b)

☐ ☐ ☐ ☐ ☐ ☐ ☐ ☐ ☐ ☐ ☐

0   1   2   3   4   5   6   7   8   9   10

22. Does your firm aim to:

a. Captivate the customer with something new

b. Impress the customer with great value every day

(a)   (b)

☐ ☐ ☐ ☐ ☐ ☐ ☐ ☐ ☐ ☐ ☐

0   1   2   3   4   5   6   7   8   9   10

23. Which is more important?

a. Designing the product or service itself

b. Designing the business system underpinning the production and delivery of the product or service

(a)   (b)

☐ ☐ ☐ ☐ ☐ ☐ ☐ ☐ ☐ ☐ ☐

0   1   2   3   4   5   6   7   8   9   10

24. Does your business aim to provide a universal product or service that is the same always and everywhere?

a. No

b. Yes

(a)   (b)

☐ ☐ ☐ ☐ ☐ ☐ ☐ ☐ ☐ ☐ ☐

0   1   2   3   4   5   6   7   8   9   10

25. What is the level of your organization's overheads (general administrative and sales expenses, marketing, product development, research and development, and so forth)?

a. High

b. Low

(a)   (b)

☐ ☐ ☐ ☐ ☐ ☐ ☐ ☐ ☐ ☐ ☐

0   1   2   3   4   5   6   7   8   9   10

Scoring

Add up the scores for all twenty-five questions. The minimum score is zero and the maximum score is 250.

As you may have realized, the scales below each question are designed so that the left-hand side represents the typical answer of a proposition-simplifier, and the right-hand side that of a price-simplifier. So, if you have added ticks to the scales on the preceding pages, you will probably see at a glance the better strategy for your organization.

For a more precise appraisal, though, this is how to interpret your total score:

0–30 Your organization is highly suited to proposition-simplifying, and not at all to price-simplifying.

31–50 Your organization is quite well suited to proposition-simplifying, but not to price-simplifying.

51–99 There is a slight leaning towards proposition-simplifying. If your organization wants to proposition-simplify, it will have to change some of its policies. Price-simplifying is probably not feasible.

100–150 There is no substantial leaning towards either form of simplifying. This is a red light — your organization is probably unsuitable for *either* strategy.

151–199 There is a slight leaning towards price-simplifying. If your organization wants to pursue this strategy, it will have to

change some of its policies. Proposition-
simplifying is probably not feasible.

200–219   Your organization is quite well suited
to price-simplifying, but not to
proposition-simplifying.

220–250   Your organization is highly well suited
to price-simplifying, and not at all to
proposition-simplifying.

The Gap Test

Business strategy — especially when it involves case studies
from business schools — is always written with the benefit
of hindsight and often with a very broad brush. It's like the
plot of an old-fashioned thriller in which the good guys and
the bad guys are sharply defined: the good guys always get
stuck in terrible fixes, but they know what they are doing and
somehow emerge victorious as the story races to its climax.

But business does not work like this. The good guys often
don't have a clue what they are doing. They try one approach,
find it doesn't work, then pivot to a different strategy, and
another, and another, until they finally find one that works.

A superb illustration of this phenomenon is the struggle
in the 1960s and 1970s between the iconic motorcycle manufacturer Harley-Davidson and the Japanese upstart Honda.
We know that Honda eventually won the war because they
price-simplified. They were able to introduce to the market
bikes that were "inferior" to those of Harley-Davidson —
lower in power and much smaller — but priced much more
competitively. According to a careful reconstruction of history
by the Boston Consulting Group — conducted for Tony Benn,

the UK's socialist Trade and Industry Minister in 1975, who wanted to explore strategy options for Britain's ailing motorcycle industry — Honda won because they adopted a different business system with much lower costs than Harley. Japanese labor productivity was far higher than that in the UK, and Honda also had much greater scale in the production of small engines. This, in turn, rested on a large domestic motorcycle market and the fact that the same engines were used in lawnmowers and other applications as well as in motorcycles. Honda started with a 50cc bike and then gradually worked its way up, eventually challenging Harley in all but the most powerful and expensive bikes. It could do this because it had much lower costs and charged much lower prices.[2]

As an interpretation of what happened, the BCG report is brilliant — superbly written, incisive economic analysis based on accurate data. As history, though, it is bunk. Because Honda actually started with the *wrong* strategy and found the right one only by accident.

Honda "knew" that its little 50cc delivery bike had no market in America, so it did not try to sell it there. Unsurprisingly, the company's market research showed that Americans liked heavy, fast, powerful bikes ... and that price was relatively unimportant to them. So Honda decided to design and make a big, relatively expensive bike. Then they sent three employees to Los Angeles to start selling it.

The whole project was a total fiasco. Most dealers refused even to stock the Honda bikes. But even worse was to come when the Honda men managed to sell a few hundred of them. Honda had no experience of making bikes that were driven over long distances on freeways, and it soon turned out that its new product was no good for this — the clutches wore out in no time and oil leaks splattered American roads. Honda conscientiously air-freighted replacement parts from Japan to the United States, but the expense of doing so nearly bankrupted the firm.

Kihachiro Kawashima had the unenviable task of leading Honda's three-man American sales and marketing team. One Saturday he sought relief from his work troubles by going dirt-biking in the hills around LA on the little "Supercub" 50cc bike he'd shipped over from Japan. The next week, he invited his colleagues to share this biking therapy. (They had had also brought over Supercubs to get around LA.) To cut a long story short, these three Dinky Toy bikes were noticed and admired by the other dirt-bikers, with many of them asking where they could buy one. The three Honda executives became convinced that they could sell the Supercub for recreational purposes, mainly for the type of off-road biking they themselves enjoyed each weekend. Head office in Japan hated the idea, because they still believed the market research which stated that chunky Americans would never buy tiny Japanese bikes. But out of sheer desperation — after the evident failure of the big-bike strategy — they eventually agreed to let Kawashima give it a go. The rest you know. The small-bike market took off, initially among off-road enthusiasts, but then with commuters and other road users, too. The U.S. motorcycle market grew from 550,000 units in 1959 to around five million a year by 1975, almost all driven by Honda's small-bike policy.[3] As the company sold more bikes, it was able to cut costs and retail price even further, and the market exploded.

The moral of this story is that Honda initially chose the wrong strategy — it targeted ground that was already well occupied by a competitor with better products. Instead, it should have aimed for a gap through price-simplifying, for which it already had the ideal product. Honda could have saved itself a great deal of money and frustration if it had asked a simple question from the outset: "Does a competent competitor already occupy the ground we plan to target?" If the answer to that question is "Yes" — as it would have been in this instance — that is always a red flag. A necessary follow-up question is: "Can we simplify to provide a product that is better in terms of usefulness, ease of use and/or art?" Unless the answer to that question is a clear "Yes," too, it is better to scrap the whole project.

Every firm should abide by two decision rules:

- If the market leader is competing on features and performance, do not try to muscle your way into its market unless and until you have simplified to provide a much superior product that is a joy to use.
- If there is a gap and no firm is occupying the price-simplifying ground, and you can think of a way to cut prices in half, go for it.

In 1931, Charles Guth bought the Pepsi-Cola Company. He was already a successful entrepreneur, but Pepsi was just a shell company, with a trademark and a formula, but no sales. Guth tried to breathe life into the brand by selling it through Loft, Inc., his chain of confectionery shops. It didn't work. Meanwhile, Coca-Cola remained totally dominant in the cola market, increasing its sales and profits even during the Great Depression.

Guth realized he had to try a new tack, so he price-simplified. He effectively halved the price of cola by selling a twelve-ounce bottle of Pepsi for a nickel, the same price as a six-ounce bottle of Coke. A radio jingle — to the tune of "Do Ye Ken John Peel" — promoted the offer throughout the country:

> *Pepsi-Cola hits the spot*
> *Twelve full ounces, that's a lot*
> *Twice as much for a nickel too*
> *Pepsi-Cola is the drink for you*

The new strategy was clever because the vast majority of the cost of a bottle of cola lies in the bottling and distribution, not in the ingredients, so the cost difference between a twelve-ounce bottle and a six-ounce bottle was relatively small. Of course, it cost a bit more to make and transport the larger bottles, but nowhere near *twice* as much. Hence the extra value for customers far exceeded the additional cost for Pepsi-Cola.

Guth's business system was pretty rudimentary, but it worked. In less than four years he built five bottling plants and a network of 313 franchised bottlers, all churning out the new bigger bottles. No other soft-drink producer moved quickly enough to copy Pepsi's strategy. Coca-Cola refused to contemplate competing on price and did not retaliate, even though, with its much larger economies of scale and far lower costs, it could easily have bankrupted Pepsi if it had chosen to create a new "fighting brand" (not Coke) to imitate its rival's strategy and undercut the price. That was a fateful decision. By 1940, Pepsi had a 10.8 percent share of the total U.S. soft-drinks market, and it was more than a fifth of the size of Coke, from a standing start less than a decade earlier. The following year, Pepsi declared a pre-tax profit of $14.9 million, which compared very respectably with the market leader's $55.2 million.[4] A one-horse race had become the two-horse race that we have witnessed ever since — and it started when Pepsi took the price-simplifying ground that Coca-Cola had ignored.

But what if there is already a mass market, yet no substantial *premium* market? If you can think of a new strategy and build a unique a new business system, occupy the vacant ground:

- If no firm is the clear leader in proposition-simplifying, and you can simplify to deliver a much better product or experience, go for it!

In 1921, Pierre du Pont, the boss of General Motors (GM), asked his vice-president of operations, Alfred Sloan, to look at product policy and work out a new strategy to compete with Ford. The prospects seemed bleak: Ford was dominant, with 62 percent of the market; GM was only a quarter the size. Indeed, its disadvantages in terms of costs and profits were even greater than this would suggest, as its volume was split between *five* separate companies, all of which competed with the others as well as with Ford.

Presented with this uninviting task, Sloan did not attempt to compete with Ford in what we would call the price-simplifying space. Instead, he pitched GM into the proposition-simplifying space. He defined new segments of the market, and tailored products for them that would excite target customers. He started by giving each of the five GM car marques a distinctive position and price range, eliminating duplication and competition for the same customers between them. This not only improved margins for GM but simplified the product image and role for the buyer. Each marque was appropriate for a different kind of buyer, based on how much he (it was nearly always a he) could afford to pay. The entry-level marque was the Chevrolet, positioned as a better — if slightly more expensive — alternative to Ford's Model T. Next came Oakland (soon to be renamed Pontiac), then Buick, then Oldsmobile, and finally, at the apex of customer aspiration, Cadillac. Customers were encouraged to trade up to whichever GM marque was positioned immediately above the one they already owned.

Sloan also introduced annual model changes. "The changes in the new model," he wrote, "should be so novel and attractive as to create demand for the new value." This he identified as a matter of style — "art," as we have defined it. "Each line of General Motors cars should preserve a distinction of appearance, so that one knows on sight a Chevrolet, a Pontiac, an Oldsmobile, a Buick, or a Cadillac." He set up a new "Art and Color Section" in Detroit and installed Harley Earl — who had previously worked in Hollywood, making custom car bodies for movie stars — as its chief. In a more modest way, Sloan wanted his cars to be a joy to own and somehow to reflect his customers' personalities. By contrast, Henry Ford, says the historian Richard Tedlow, "made no concession to consumer self-expression ... he felt so strongly that people *should not* want anything other than basic transportation."[5]

Sloan also improved ease of use for drivers and product utility, adding new features such as gear shifters and shock absorbers as standard, features that Ford's Model T did not boast.[6] Finally, he facilitated purchase by extending credit to both customers and dealers — making GM the first carmaker to offer this. Local dealers immediately lined up to defect from the frugal Ford system to the more open-handed GM one, which resulted in a massive increase in the quality and quantity of the company's dealer network. This was especially important for GM's trade-in/trade-up policy, which Ford, still with just one basic model, could not emulate. Sloan courted the dealers assiduously, asking for feedback on GM's products and plans, and on customer attitudes. He even had a special railroad car fitted out as an office, so that he and his team could visit every dealer in a city in turn.[7]

By doing the opposite of Ford, GM not only occupied the product proposition space but gained overall market leadership in 1931, a position it then kept for the next seventy-seven years. It finally lost the top spot in 2007 to another proposition-simplifier, Toyota, which, just as GM had done decades earlier, offered a simpler range and a much higher-quality product. In 2008, GM sold nine different vehicles that were all priced at $25,500. Toyota offered just two.[8]

So, we can restate the lesson in one rule:

- Go for the gap — and do the opposite from the market leader before anyone else does.

This bring us on to our next test.

The Keys Test

Successful simplifiers always come up with a new key, or keys, to unlock and transform a market. These keys are almost never based on market research. Instead, they come from *insight* — often a sudden epiphany or a bolt from the blue that nearly always arrives away from the office. But one of our aims in this book is to simplify and systematize insight. We believe that by studying previous conceptual breakthroughs, it is possible to emulate them and adapt them for a new context.

A striking finding of our research is that certain patterns keep recurring in the most successful simplification stories. Though there might be one initial key that unlocks the imagination — Ingvar Kamprad chopping off the legs of a table to stuff it into his car boot; the McDonald brothers applying the industrial assembly-line process to their restaurant — usually that key leads to another, then a third, and a fourth. So there is usually a *cluster of keys*.

Another finding is that the keys for the two main types of simplifying are different, yet similar within each type. When you think about it, this is not surprising. Just as there are said to be only seven basic plots for a successful novel, there are only a handful of ways to achieve the objective of price-simplifying, and a different handful of ways to meet the contrasting aims of proposition-simplifiers.

Keys in Price-Simplifying

The sole objective of price-simplifiers is to cut costs by at least half. In our case studies we have already come across the main keys they use to achieve this:

- Ford: Reduce variety, redesign product, introduce new production system (massive investment and invention of the assembly line), use better-quality materials.
- IKEA: Redesign products, control furniture-makers, reduce variety, build giant stores, co-opt customers (self-service, self-delivery, self-assembly).

- McDonald's: Reduce variety, automate, speed up service, co-opt customers and franchisees, use better-quality ingredients.
- Penguin: Reduce variety, create new distribution channels, raise quality of content, lower overheads, co-opt authors and other publishers.
- Honda: Reduce variety, scale down product, lower costs of labor and of the main component (the engine).
- Pepsi-Cola: Offer twice as much product for the same price, use effective advertising, introduce new distribution system, exploit market leader's price umbrella.

These themes consistently recur in the case studies we will discuss later in this book.

Keys in Proposition-Simplifying

The aim of the proposition-simplifier is to make the product or service a joy to use by increasing ease of use, usefulness and art. We have seen examples of the following keys so far:

- Apple Macintosh: Create high-end customer segment, make product more intuitive for the user, design a user-friendly and beautiful item that is also more useful than existing machines.
- Uber: Make experience of using a taxi quicker, more friendly and more reliable, and also often cheaper, through new software.
- BCG: Create new high-end "strategy" product (the first new consulting product since the introduction of "time and motion"), condense ideas, so that devising

strategy becomes memorable and fun, select a few principles so that any properly trained person can use them, communicate shared framework throughout the firm, prioritize actions and standardize projects.

- Bain & Company: Create new high-end "CEO" service, co-opt the CEO, increase ease of profit improvement throughout the client firm, increase usefulness of consulting process.

- General Motors: Create new segments in middle and top of the market, each targeted at different customers and with different styles and appearance, raise customer utility through brand differentiation and new annual models, introduce new features to make cars a joy to drive, and raise ease of purchase for customers and dealers by extending credit.

If you can see a key, does it belong to price- or proposition-simplifying? That will give you at least a clue as to the better strategy for you.

Now for our final test.

The Better Skills Test

In order to succeed as a simplifier, your firm needs to have the right skill set for your market, but it must also be *better* at simplifying in that way than any current or potential competitor. This is a hard test for companies and it is easy for them to delude themselves, or to miss one vital skill that they don't possess while some other firm does.

Think back to the personal computer war of the 1980s and 1990s — a war whose effects we are still feeling today, not least because it crippled not one but two giant corporations (IBM and Xerox) and was crucial in the rise of another firm (Apple), which may prove to be the biggest and longest-running success story of our era.

First, let's think about what happened to Xerox. That corporation — or rather a spin-off from it — could have become the most valuable in the world from the 1980s onwards. The computer scientists at Xerox PARC invented the modern PC and much else besides. They can lay claim to developing the desktop and the mouse, and they could — perhaps should — have been able to claim the power and the glory, too. Imagine for a moment what would have happened if Steve Jobs — who was hugely impressed by what he saw at Xerox PARC in 1979 — had decided to throw in his lot with the company. Imagine what would have happened if the leaders of the copier-company back at HQ in New York State had enjoyed a collective fit of intelligence and decided to buy Apple. They could have funded such an acquisition out of their petty cash. Imagine what would have happened if the Xerox bosses had been properly advised, if they had merged Xerox PARC and Apple — they were close both geographically and spiritually — if they had put Jobs in charge of "Xerox Apple," if they had then spun it off to Xerox shareholders as a separately quoted company, with Jobs and his pals as substantial shareholders in the new entity. And imagine if Jobs — while clearly the *numero uno* — had agreed to hire a world-class CEO or COO to handle the hard job of managing the technological prima donnas — and that the two bosses had then got along famously.

It's a lot to imagine. Yet, what fireworks the world would have seen. Xerox's cash coupled with Apple and Xerox

PARC's expertise would surely have delivered a terrific second-generation PC — complete with desktop, mouse, smooth scrolling, and plenty of power — not in the late 1980s (when the Mac finally achieved the feat), but in 1981 or 1982 *at the latest*. If that had happened, Jobs never would have been thrown out of Apple, and "Xerox Apple" would not have messed around with the Newton, but instead would have moved on to the brave new world of the iPod, the iPhone and the iPad in the 1990s, rather than the 2000s. Much of the top talent in Silicon Valley would surely have gravitated towards "Xerox Apple." And Steve Jobs, not Bill Gates, would have become the richest person in the world.

History tells a different story, though. On its own, Xerox PARC utterly failed to capitalize on its discoveries. There were two reasons for this. First, the research unit had weak or non-existent commercial skills, and no other department within Xerox had them, either. True, excellent product management skills could have been employed, but a head office that did not understand the need for them was never likely to do that — and it didn't! The Xerox HQ probably subtracted more shareholder value than any other head office in the last century by not understanding the potential gold mine it possessed out in California.

Second, and more fundamentally, the folks at Xerox PARC did not have the simplifying mentality of Steve Jobs. They did not understand the importance of ease of use. If they had, they would have made their mouse far easier to use, would have cracked the issue of smooth scrolling, and would have commercialized their version of WYSIWYG much more quickly. Nor did they think to make their machine as useful as it could be, or understand the importance of a slick appearance and a stylish design. This was because they never viewed the computer as a consumer product.

In short, the Xerox PARC engineers — brilliant and trail-blazing innovators though they were — did not share Steve Jobs' vision of a simple product. They easily comprehended, and rather relished, the complexity with which they wrestled every day. By contrast, they had no interest in simplifying. They snatched defeat from the jaws of victory because they liked complexity more than they liked simplicity. Anyone who has compared the Xerox Star with the Macintosh knows this to be true. The former was clunky, over-engineered and hard to use; the latter was intuitive, elegant and, once it had sufficient power, a joy to use.

And what about IBM? It was not a natural price-simplifier. It never aimed to provide the cheapest PC on the market, nor even the cheapest "quality" PC. And it was hobbled by being a high-overhead company. But was it a proposition-simplifier, or *could* it have become one?

If we propel ourselves back to the early 1980s again, we might argue that IBM set the standard in PCs, and did so by simplifying. As we saw earlier, it introduced its PC in 1981, and within two years it commanded a full quarter of the market, easily outselling the Apple II. Yet, from the moment the Macintosh arrived in 1984, it was clear that IBM had lost the proposition high ground because the Apple's operating system was so much easier to use. IBM scrambled around in alliance with Microsoft to produce its Windows equivalent, but it never caught up. True, IBM continued to outsell Apple by a wide margin for many years, but Apple kept the premium market in its pocket, as a higher-value and more profitable business as IBM continued to lose money on each and every PC it sold.

IBM should have gone one of two ways: either produce a machine that was clearly superior to the Mac (i.e. more useful, easier to use, and more aesthetically appealing) or sell the lowest-price machine by some distance. It did neither. Instead, it remained stuck in the middle, outflanked by Apple at the top and by Hewlett-Packard, Compaq, and Dell in the mass market.

But were the better options ever really options at all? In the premium market, IBM would have succeeded only by buying Apple and then allowing a "reverse takeover," whereby the leaders of the puny Apple would have been handed the reins of the mighty IBM. Such a scenario was always extremely improbable. So what about the mass market? For sure, IBM could have insisted that Microsoft — then a small company that relied on its association with IBM — not license its Windows software to other computer manufacturers. But IBM would still have been constrained by its high-cost structure — its successful sales force and matchless technical support — and its customer base, which was confined mainly to large and some medium-sized companies. It is hard to believe that HP, Compaq, Dell, or another company would not have found a way around the software problem — possibly by sponsoring one of Microsoft's rivals — and then leapfrogged IBM by selling direct to customers, rendering IBM's highly paid sales force a liability rather than an asset.

One possible salvation for IBM might have been to scour the world for the lowest-cost PC manufacturer and outsource all its manufacturing, closing its U.S. factories, dismantling its sales team and adopting the Dell model of direct selling. But then, of course, IBM would not have been IBM.

The simplicity tests outlined above would have indicated

in no uncertain terms that IBM's position was hopeless right from the start (without desperate measures and complete transformation), because it faced one rival that was more skilled at proposition-simplifying and several others that were more skilled at price-simplifying.

So the Skills Test is vital, although it can be extremely tough for management to accept. In some circumstances, deliverance can come only from a dissident management faction, or from investors insisting on radical action. Yet it must be understood and widely employed. Nobody in the late 1970s or early 1980s realized that IBM was set to fail. Yet if the company's bosses had explored whether they were able to pursue either form of simplifying better than their rivals they would have seen the writing on the wall. Similar analysis could be employed in some of the world's most valuable companies today, and it would undoubtedly show that several of them are set to fail, too.

Key Points

1. Take the Attitude Test. See whether your firm is a "natural" price- or proposition-simplifier.

2. The Gap Test asks you if there is already a price-simplifier or proposition-simplifier in your market. If your firm's natural direction is vacant in the market, seize the ground. If it is occupied, beware.

3. The Keys Test invites you to find a cluster of keys that might unlock a simplifying opportunity. The best clues may be what previous very successful simplifiers of your type did in other markets.

4. The Better Skills Test explains that, to succeed in the

long run, your company must have the skills to execute one of the two simplifying strategies but must also possess those skills to a higher degree than any competitor. Do you think that it meets these criteria?

5. If these tests all point in the same direction, your strategy is internally consistent and makes sense. Taken together, these are hard tests to pass. If your firm fails them, you should assess how it might be protected against a radical price- or proposition-simplifier. And if the odds of that do not look good, perhaps you should consider moving to another firm — one that has a great simplifying opportunity. If you are an investor, you may wish to do the same.

You should now have decided whether your firm should — and has the ability to — become a price-simplifier or a proposition-simplifier. But how exactly do you become one of these two types of simplifier? The next three chapters will provide the answer.

9

How to Proposition-Simplify

You need a very product-oriented culture.[1]

Steve Jobs

A good taxi driver may be 2 or 3 times better than a bad one. But a good designer is 100 or 200 times better.[2]

Steve Jobs

Good design is as little design as possible.

Dieter Rams

Product design is nearly everything in proposition-simplifying. The objective is to make the product a joy to use: first and foremost, *easier to use*; then, if possible, *more useful* and *more aesthetically appealing.*

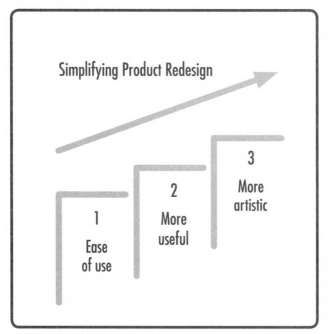

Figure 2: Three steps to start a proposition revolution

If a new product or service is more useful and artistic than rival products but does not make life easier for the user, then there has been no proposition-simplifying. The product may be wonderful, but the ideas in this book probably will not apply to it. For example, the Porsche 911, introduced in 1963, gave a different driving experience from that of any comparable sports car. It was also a work of art. But the 911 did *not* make driving easier; probably the reverse, because, with its rear-mounted engine and unusual weight distribution, it required considerable skill to drive. Aficionados may see that as part of its appeal, but it disqualifies it from being a form of proposition-simplifying. Nor was the 911 any easier or cheaper to make than comparable cars, so it was not an example of price-simplifying, either. In general, simplifying is neither necessary nor natural for luxury products, such as Porsche cars and Rolex watches. Luxury markets are not price sensitive, and complexity is often part of the appeal of the product.

By our definition, *all* examples of successful proposition-simplifying involve increasing ease of use. This attribute is the most important in leading to greater customer adoption — if a product or service is easier to use, more people will use it. This is invariably the case, whereas proposition-simplifying does not always involve making a product more useful and/or more aesthetically appealing (although this often happens too).

Step One: Easier to Use

The essential first step — make the user experience easy and simple — is more than the sum of its parts. It requires empathy with the user and a genuine simplifying mission.

Who do you think would make the better designer of electronic devices? Someone with a natural affinity for computers, even back in the day when operating them required real skill? Or someone who found that experience extremely tough? Listen to one of the latter:

> "I went right through college having a real problem with computers. I was convinced I was technically inept ... Right at the end of my time as a student I discovered the Mac. I remember being astounded at how much better it was ... I was struck by the care taken with the whole user experience. I had a sense of connection via the object with the designers."[3]

The speaker was Jony Ive, the son of a London silversmith. He went on to become a product designer and was the man behind the iMac, MacBook Air, iPod, iPhone, iPad and Apple Watch. If we look at how these devices (and those in our other simplifying case studies) were made easier to use, we see five major themes:

- eliminate;
- make intuitive and easier;
- make faster;
- make smaller/lighter/more portable;
- make easier to obtain.

Eliminate

Remember that Steve Jobs "made devices simpler by eliminating buttons, software simpler by eliminating features, and interfaces simpler by eliminating options." In designing the Mac, he eliminated all the function keys and cursor arrows, features that all other computer manufacturers thought were essential. Users were forced to use the mouse instead, which they soon learned was a much more elegant way to move the cursor around the screen, once they got used to it. Ive, whom Jobs called his "spiritual partner," also started his career at Apple by eliminating. "We wanted to get rid of anything other than what was absolutely essential," he said. "We kept going back to the beginning again and again, "Do we need that part? Can we get it to perform the function of the other four parts?" It became an exercise to reduce and reduce, but it makes it easier to build and easier for people to work."[4]

Intuitive and Easier

Simplicity for the user is complexity concealed. Ive says he aims "to solve incredibly complex problems and make their resolution appear inevitable and incredibly simple [to the user], so that you have no sense how difficult this thing was."[5] The iPad is a superb illustration. Have you sat in a doctor's waiting room or on a plane and seen a toddler playing games or watching cartoons on an iPad? It is literally child's play. No stumbling blocks — no causes of possible frustration — are allowed on the device, which is the reason why you can't print from it.

Faster

Almost every device is getting ever faster to use, but some are faster than others — faster to boot up, faster to operate, faster to service. Products and services can create a new market or niche they then dominate for decades merely by performing an operation much faster than their rivals. The Polaroid instant camera was introduced in 1948, and the Polaroid Corporation then dominated the market for four decades, selling 14.3 million cameras in 1978 alone. Eventually, of course, it was superseded by the digital camera.

Today, AUTO1.com lets Europeans sell their cars quickly and easily by making a cash-up-front offer to buy them, and at the same time gives car dealers access to inventory delivered within hours. Bringing rapid network efficiency to the used-car trade has helped create one of Europe's fastest growing businesses, backed by the authors.

Nespresso is another prime example. Its machines make high-quality coffee far faster than any rival system of comparable quality. They are also simple to use, stylish, and cleaning them is a doddle.

Smaller/Lighter/More Portable

The Walkman, introduced by Akio Morita's Sony Corporation in 1979, was easier to use than other cassette players, but the big advance was its portability. Previously, people would walk down the street with huge boom-boxes perched on their shoulders. The Walkman subtracted the integral loudspeakers, replacing them with small headphones, as well as the ability to record. As a result, and by using its in-house technicians' genius for miniaturization, it was possible to make a thin and light machine that could be carried anywhere. The Walkman also played magnetic tapes, meaning it had superior sound quality than rival formats, even though the machine was much lighter and more compact. In the face of stiff competition from Toshiba, Aiwa, and Panasonic, the Sony device remained dominant in its segment and highly profitable until the late 1990s. It declined only when the iPod and iTunes took over by reinventing and transcending all the advantages of ease of use, miniaturization, and portability.

Easier to Obtain

iTunes also made music much easier to buy. It was no longer necessary to make a trip to the record store, album tracks could be purchased individually for the first time, and users could choose from a much wider selection than any record store could possibly stock. Spotify has since taken this process a step further by giving its users instant access to millions of songs through streaming.

Of course, making products easier to obtain is not a new idea: as we saw earlier, in the 1920s General Motors introduced credit for customers who wished to trade up to more expensive cars. But there are always new means to make a product more accessible. Unlike traditional car rental firms, Zipcar — founded in 2000 — allows its customers to rent vehicles by the hour, and it prides itself on making the whole hiring process quick and hassle-free. It operates on a membership model: once you become a member you can unlock the car using your membership card or a mobile phone and drive away within seconds. The cars are also parked in street-side bays, closer to most customers than the majority of car rental offices. Avis Budget Group acquired Zipcar in 2014 for around half a billion dollars.

The dramatic and controversial success of Wonga, provider of "pay day" loans in the UK, Europe, Canada, and South Africa, is based on the company making cash advances much easier for qualified applicants to obtain. Wonga greatly simplified the whole process of securing a short-term loan and then paying the principal and (very high) interest back to the company over the next few weeks. Indeed, regulators have argued that Wonga not only charges excessive interest rates but has made loans *too easy* to obtain. Recently, the UK and other countries have introduced caps on the interest such firms may charge.

Step Two: More Useful

There are also five ways to make a product or service more *useful*:

- vary performance — make more (or less) powerful;
- improve quality;
- add new capabilities without adversely affecting ease of use;
- provide a wider range of products;[6] and
- personalize.

Some propositions are more useful across all five of these dimensions. For example:

- Facebook offers a "social operating system" for the internet, aiming to sit at the center of users' online social lives.[7] You could argue that it ticks all the boxes above when compared with how people traditionally kept in touch and interacted, and that it offers a wide range of activities on the site while ensuring that it remains easy to use.
- TripAdvisor, Google Search, and Uber also tick all five boxes, as did General Motors in the 1920s.

Other propositions tick most of the boxes:

- BCG provided an original decision-making framework — the famous Boston Box with its cows, dogs, stars, and question-marks — that was much simpler than anything that had been devised before. It was also more powerful, higher quality, enabled a company to monitor a new capability (relative market share), and allowed the matrix to be personalized to the company's exact position.

In some cases, however, one or two of the ways to increase usefulness stand out:

- Starbucks' usefulness hinges on the fact that it is a convenient place to meet friends, with pleasant surroundings. You won't be moved on as soon as you've finished your drink and the wifi is free. Oh yes, and they sell a wide range of coffee (although the quality is hotly debated).
- The Sony Walkman was more useful mainly because of its superior sound quality. Apart from this, the enhancement in usefulness was limited; the big attraction, as we noted earlier, was in ease of use through portability.

Although greater usefulness is present in the large majority of proposition-simplifying examples, in some cases it is not important at all. With Wonga and Zipcar, for instance, ease of use (specifically the ease with which the product may be obtained) is paramount; the basic *usefulness* of the product (short-term loans and car hire, respectively) has hardly changed at all.

Figure 3 illustrates the ways in which certain companies and products have increased usefulness. Does it prompt any ideas with respect to your own product or service?

The signature characteristic of proposition-simplifiers is that, in all cases, hard usefulness is added without making the user experience more complicated. Moreover, boosts to

	Improve Performance	Improve Quality	Improve Capabilities	Wider Range	Personalize
General Motors	●	●	●	●	●
Transistor Radio	—	—	—	—	—
Sony Digital Camera	●	●	●	—	●
Dyson Bagless VC	●	—	—	—	—
Nespresso		●		●	
Nintendo Wii	●	—	●	—	—
Macintosh PC	●	●	●	—	◑
iPod	●	●	●	—	●
iPhone	●	●	●	—	●
iPad	●	●	●	—	●
Google Search	●	●	●	●	●
Google Maps	—	—	●	●	●
TripAdvisor		●	●	●	●
Facebook	●	●	●	●	●
Wonga	—	—	—	—	—
Sony Walkman	—	●	—	—	●
Starbucks		●		●	
eBay	—	—	●	●	●
Twitter	—	—	●	●	●
BCG	●	●	●	—	●
Bain & Co	●	●	—	—	●
Uber	●	●	●	●	●
Zipcar	—	—	—	—	—

Figure 3: Innovations employed by some proposition-simplifiers to make their products more useful

the product's usefulness are always combined with increases in its ease of use.

Step Three: More Aesthetically Appealing

As you will recall, we define "art" as anything that enhances the *appeal* of a product that cannot be reduced to hard usefulness or ease of use. Art is to do with the appearance and texture of a product or service, how it makes the customer feel, and how it turns consumption into a great experience.

Steve Jobs understood this better than anyone. When making the Apple II, he took inspiration from Cuisinart's revolutionary food processor, introduced five years earlier. With its rounded, transparent shapes, the Cuisinart is very useful but also a beautiful artefact in itself. Jobs repeatedly told his people to make Apple computers "look friendly." Hardly anyone understood what he meant, but that was part of the advantage he had over his rivals. It is hard to imagine IBM's designers — competent as they were — understanding the concept of a "warm and friendly" machine. Jobs explained: "We're really shooting for Museum of Modern Art quality."[8] He urged this principle to be applied even to invisible components, such as the motherboard: "I want it to be as beautiful as possible, even if it's inside the box. A great carpenter isn't going to use lousy wood for the back of the cabinet, even though nobody's going to see it."[9] First impressions were crucial: "When you open the box of an iPhone or iPad, we want that tactile experience to set the tone for how you perceive the product."[10]

More than nine out of every ten proposition-simplifying cases we have identified have involved a substantial addition of art to the product mix. One of the earliest examples was Alfred Sloan's decision to change General Motors' car models every year — the first time anyone in the industry had displayed such a commitment to style and fashion. "The appearance of a motorcar," he said, "is a most important factor ... perhaps the most important single factor."[11]

Today, web-based companies such as Google, Twitter, and Spotify lavish a great deal of attention on how they present themselves. In a prophetic article in the *New York Times* in 2007 — when Myspace was three times larger than Facebook — the latter's "clean, uniform appearance" was contrasted with the former's cluttered layout. A user of both said that he checked Facebook several times every day but hardly look at his Myspace account any more. "Myspace is so messy and there's so much spam. It's not worth it," he said.[12]

Art can simplify or it can make a product more complicated. You should aim for the kind that simplifies, that communicates so directly and intuitively that words and other explanations become redundant. With the desktop icons on the first Macintosh, and the touch-screen capability of the iPod, iPhone, and iPad, we see a marriage of art and technology that not only beguiles users but makes their lives easier and richer. The best simplifying art is important not only in its own right but because of the hard benefits it generates in terms of convenience and utility.

The Vespa scooter shows how art can combine seamlessly with ease of use. Introduced in 1946, conceived to be both a work of art and an intensely practical machine, it was designed to be extremely easy to use for its well-dressed riders. Men in suits and women in ankle-length skirts were able to ride the scooters without any risk to their expensive clothes. The patent documentation said the motorcycle had a frame "with mudguards and engine cowling covering all working parts" so that it would offer "protection from mud and dust without jeopardizing requirements of appearance and elegance." In the 1953 movie *Roman Holiday*, Audrey Hepburn rides side-saddle on Gregory Peck's Vespa. In the sixties it was still a style icon, publicized by the Beatles and featuring in Fellini's *La Dolce Vita*.

Another product that uses art to reinforce ease of use and practical value is the Dyson bagless cleaner. It is easier to use than a conventional vacuum cleaner because there is no bag to replace. It advanced performance through its patented cyclonic separation technology. And it embodies simplifying art by letting you see what it is picking up, so you realize what a good job it is doing.

So, art is usually a very important element in any proposition, but it can vary enormously from product to product. Whichever form it takes, though, the "artists" and designers who are given the task of creating a new product should understand clearly that their mission is both to simplify and to make that product a joy to use. Therefore, hire the best creative talent you can afford, and ensure that they really love the product before you commission them.

Are Free Services Price- or Proposition-Simplifying?

Cutting the price of a service to zero might seem like an extreme form of price-simplifying. But, of course, the zero price is always an illusion. Free isn't really free; free is a trade.

There are two common models of this. One is when the consumer is offered a service at zero price but the supplier's business model relies upon selling advertising. Here, the supplier is buying the attention of the consumer and selling this attention to third parties. Social media companies such as Facebook and Twitter use this model, as does Google Search, albeit in a slightly different way. It's a very old model, stretching back to the first days of newspapers, commercial radio, and television.

The other option is the "freemium" model, where a basic service is provided free to all subscribers, but premium services incur a fee. This model can be seen in a wide variety of consumer and business software-as-a-service models, from dating sites such as Tinder, to Dropbox and Spotify, to newspaper and magazine websites. Most users prefer to pay nothing and put up with the basic service, but successful companies attract enough premium subscribers to make their businesses profitable. Of course, the "free" price is illusory for those who try for free and then decide to pay for the premium service.

The basis of competition is not price, but proposition. The winning dating site is the one that offers the most attractive service to its target market. The winning search engine is the one that most users choose to use because they like the way it works. And this is facilitated by our three (not free) friends — making the service easier to use, making it more useful, and making it more aesthetically appealing. The rules for free services are precisely the same as those for any other form of proposition-simplifying. The fact that the service can be free — for a certain group of participants — facilitates entry to the market and allows a large and potentially valuable network to be built, packaged and sold to a different set of customers.

Conclusion

To proposition-simplify, you need to provide a product that is a cut above others on the basis of three criteria — make it easier to use, more useful and more emotionally appealing. If you can do that, you will enjoy both high growth and high margins, which in turn will lead to significant increases in cash flow and company valuation. The jackpot comes when proposition-simplifying spawns a new mass market. When Steve Jobs returned to Apple in 1997 and resumed the process of proposition-simplifying, the firm was valued at $2.25 billion. At the time of writing, Apple was worth $742 billion — 330 times more.

The Achilles heel of proposition-simplifying is that it can be hard to fend off imitators, or new proposition-simplifiers who come up with unique and even more compelling products. Proposition-simplifying is an innovation treadmill, and very few firms stay on it for more than a decade or two. These days, breakthrough products may enjoy only five years in the sun before they are reverse engineered, imitated, and forfeit both market share and margin. Hence, even successful proposition-simplifiers often achieve a stratospheric market value only eventually to plunge back to earth. The problem is defensibility, or rather the lack of it. On the other hand, as we saw with McKinsey, BCG, and Bain, proposition-simplifying can lead to subtly differentiated competition, with several firms able to lead within their own segments and all generating huge profits in what outsiders perceive to be a single market (whereas in fact it is nothing of the sort).

Price-simplifying works differently. It generates much lower margins, but greater defensibility. That is why many of the most successful price-simplifying firms have been at the top for many years. It is not unusual to see price-simplifiers such as McDonald's, IKEA, and the budget airlines increasing their market share steadily over time, and they tend to be far more competitively secure than many proposition-simplifiers. The reason for this is that, in addition to undertaking radical *product* redesign, price-simplifiers redesign the whole *business system* to attain a low-cost position that simply cannot be challenged by competitors and to erect extra defenses that protect the business over the long term. In the next chapter we explain how they do this.

Key Points

1. The heart of proposition-simplifying is total product or service redesign — your simplifying should be radical, so that the product is easier to use, more useful, and more beautiful.
2. The trick is to increase *ease of use*, making the product a joy to use. The five best ways to achieve this are to: eliminate superfluous features and components; make it intuitive to use; make it faster; make it smaller, lighter and/or more portable; and make it easier to access.
3. Make the product *more useful* without making it harder to use; greater utility without greater ease of use is pointless.
4. *Art* — the emotional connection to the user — is the third weapon in your armory. The best art not only impresses but makes the product more intuitive.
5. Proposition-simplifying can lead to huge increases in sales and profits, perhaps sustained over a decade

or more. But the greatest challenge is to stay ahead of imitators. The timescale for enjoying a secure lead with new products appears to be decreasing, so constant innovation is necessary for sustained success. The greatest danger is that the innovator's creative wellsprings become exhausted.

10

How to Price-Simplify
Part I: Product Redesign

I can teach you the secret to running this airline in thirty seconds. This is it: We are THE low-fare airline.

Herb Kelleher

C an you remember when full-service airlines, with two or three classes of passengers, were the only choice — for both intercontinental *and* domestic travel? It was not a bad system, but it was complex, expensive, and exclusive. Only the rich traveled by air. Then one man changed the system forever. In this chapter, we explain how he did it, and start to explore how to create a mass market for any product that excludes most people because it is too expensive. Part of that process involves product redesign.

There is a recurring pattern with markets and firms. Companies provide better products and more of them. Striving to increase product performance multiplies both product and organizational complexity, making it harder for many customers to afford or use the product or service easily. When firms become more complex, they distance themselves from their customers, executives lose sight of what they should be doing, and products become even more elaborate and expensive. Then the music stops. One or two new entrants decide to simplify and slash prices. The new product or service they offer is often technically inferior but simpler and *much* cheaper (between 50 and 90 percent cheaper than its rivals). Demand explodes and the industry changes forever.

Airlines are a perfect example of this phenomenon. Commercial airlines emerged after the First World War, with firms such as Imperial Airways, BOAC, and BEA — which later merged to become British Airways — providing an elaborate "hub and spoke" route network that traversed the globe. Passengers could fly anywhere on a single ticket, with bags checked through to their final destination. They boarded a host of different aircraft depending on demand and location. There were several different classes of travel, all the way up to luxurious lounges that served copious meals on bone china and champagne in crystal glasses. The number of routes and standards of service rose continually, but the business system became ever more complicated and expensive to operate. This greater complexity necessitated higher fares, which were introduced, yet no airline was particularly profitable, and many suffered heavy losses for years. A mass market for air travel remained elusive.

This pattern was rudely interrupted in 1971, when Herb Kelleher started the first budget airline — Southwest — which flew a short triangular route between the Texan cities of Dallas, Houston, and San Antonio.[1] Southwest Airlines now flies more passengers within the United States than any other airline.[2]

So what was Kelleher's ticket to success?

He price-simplified by totally redesigning the product.

After declaring, "I can teach you the secret to running this airline in thirty seconds. This is it: We are THE low-fare airline," he added, "Once you understand that fact, you can make any decision about this company's future as well as I can."[3]

Kelleher was being modest. He simplified Southwest's product in several crucial ways, including:

- only point-to-point routes;
- one class of travel;
- no free refreshments or lounges;
- a fleet consisting solely of Boeing 737s, simplifying maintenance, scheduling, and training;
- ten-minute turnaround at the gate;
- utilize smaller, secondary airports, which are cheaper and faster than the main hub airports; and
- sell direct to customers.

The system worked because low prices meant the planes were usually full and costs were pared to the bone.

But behind Kelleher's product redesign lay something even more fundamental. He *automated* flying, just as Henry Ford automated car-making, Ingvar Kamprad automated the furniture industry, and the McDonald brothers automated hamburgers. We will discuss this in detail in the next chapter.

European budget airlines have further simplified Kelleher's template by co-opting customers to do some of the work, such as checking in online, carrying their own bags to the plane, and ensuring they are ready to board promptly. This creates an efficiency saving that is shared between the customers themselves and the airline.

But how do customers benefit from this efficiency saving? The obvious answer is in the price they pay: on a per mile basis, a budget airline flight is typically less than half the price of a full-service economy (coach) equivalent, and sometimes as little as a tenth. Moreover, because of fast turnaround times and the use of smaller airports, customers may also benefit from substantial time savings.

What works for the customers also works for the budget carriers. For decades the airline industry was notorious for losses and bankruptcies, and poor returns even for the survivors. Yet the largest budget airlines — Southwest, EasyJet, and Ryanair — have all demonstrated dramatic growth in revenues, earnings per share and stock market value.

Much more important, however, is that airline simplifying has made it easier for a wide range of people to visit their friends and family. It has shrunk the globe, enhancing the experiences and increasing the sophistication of hundreds of million travelers. Finally, because flying is so much safer than driving, it may even be said that the budget airlines have saved thousands of lives.

How to Spark a Price Revolution

As we know, with price-simplifying, price is everything. Price is the *strategy*. Everything else is *tactics* — the means to arrive at the target price. Price-simplifying rests on the observation that if you can halve the price, the market will more than double (and may well increase by ten times or more). And if you can somehow engineer a 75 percent reduction, the market will explode. So everything you do from now on — in thinking, in planning, and in execution — *must* be done with price in mind. It must become a burning obsession ... but for a purpose.

Even with a clear price target, it is an abstraction until you relate it to your future customers — those who are currently denied the product because it is too expensive. With price-simplifying, you are on the side of these target customers who want to buy the product or service but simply cannot afford it. Put yourself in their shoes and provide your product for a fraction of the current price.

The most effective and successful price-simplifiers think of what they do as a mission, a crusade to bring at least some of the good life to people who have not been able to afford it before. Henry Ford aimed to democratize the automobile and then did just that. Michael Marks, a Jewish refugee who fled the pogroms in tsarist Russia, and Tom Spencer, his English partner, set out to provide middle-class clothing at a price working-class people could afford. As a result of their efforts, Marks & Spencer became one of the world's most successful retailers. Herb Kelleher aimed to make flying cheaper than driving in order to create a new mass market, and he managed to do both.

If you are contemplating cutting prices in half — and perhaps in half again — you probably know that this is not "business as usual." It cannot be achieved through the usual methods. Three fundamental changes must take place:

- The *product* must be redesigned to make it simpler and cheaper. Visualize your target customers — those whom you wish to create and reward.
- The *business system* must be redesigned to make the product simpler and cheaper to produce and deliver, and to provide protection for your firm against imitators.
- The business must be *scaled* — that is, its sales must multiply, and continue to multiply — as quickly and extensively as possible.

We will now explain how you can accomplish all of this.

We have examined the most successful price-simplifiers' strategies and have summarized them in nine steps (see Figure 4). Steps One to Three relate to *product redesign*, Steps Four to Eight relate to *business system redesign*, and Step Nine relates to *scaling up your business*.

We will describe the first three steps in this chapter, and the remaining six steps in Chapter 11.

Redesign the Product

Almost anyone can think up an idea. The thing that counts is developing it into a practical product.[4]

Henry Ford

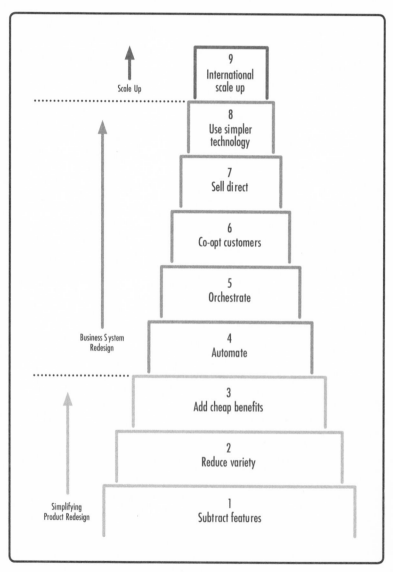

Figure 4: Nine steps to spark a price revolution

SIMPLIFY

Step One: Subtract Features/Performance and Return to the Product's Core Function

To launch a price revolution you need to work out the *core, primary function* that the product serves. Most likely the products that are currently available, before your price revolution, have strayed beyond the original purpose and now serve more than one function. For example, air travel originally aimed to cover distances faster than was possible by road, rail, or sea. But airlines quickly overlaid this utilitarian function with many other features. Even early posters advertising air travel emphasized the pleasure, romance, service, food and drink, and sophistication of flying, rather than the speed. Pleasure was added to utility, but soon threatened to eclipse it.

Sparking a price revolution in air travel therefore required going back to basics, returning to the core function — getting passengers from A to B quickly and safely. That required reliable planes and experienced crews. Nothing else: no complimentary food and drink, no lounges, no checked-through baggage, no airport check-ins, no travel agents, no allocated seats, no expensive airports.

Herb Kelleher offered a seat, not a pleasurable experience. It was air travel stripped down to the bare essentials. As he said, Southwest "is THE low-cost airline." So, he continued, if Tracy from marketing were to suggest serving a nice Caesar salad on every flight, you had to ask, "Will that help us to be THE low-cost airline?" The answer was obvious.

It was the same with Henry Ford's price revolution. All previous non-commercial vehicles had been sold as "pleasure cars" for rich enthusiasts. Ford went back to the primary function of the motor car — fast mobility. He quipped that market research was bunk because if he'd asked the public what they wanted, they'd have said "a faster horse." But that was precisely what the Model T provided. It was not a car to show off in, not a car to test your skill, not a car with a throaty roar and rapid acceleration — but it did enable millions of people to travel distances they had never dreamed possible.

With IKEA, buying a sofa or a table is not a rite of passage, not a signal that you have arrived or established independence from your parents. It is a monetary transaction, pure and simple. You don't want advice from a salesperson, don't want to bounce up and down on the sofa, don't need to know if you can get it in yellow polka-dots or brown leather. You buy it because you need it. With eBay, auctions are not some kind of upper-class ritual marked by discreet hand signals and the thrill of the chase. They are a way to buy or sell goods cheaply and quickly. With McDonald's, you do not demand a wide assortment of food, candlelight, a man in a tuxedo, a friendly waitress, or even somewhere to sit down. You want a quick, tasty, filling meal. Romance is thrown out of the window; hard utility is everything.

Every price revolution goes back to basics, back to economics, back to utility. If you are clear about a product's core function — and about everything that is *not* its core function — you are well primed for product redesign. Many of the features and services that everyone once viewed as essential fall by the wayside, and as a result some customers will be lost. Trade-offs usually involve dropping features and/or customers to get the price as low as possible.

Subtract everything that is not *absolutely* essential for a product's usefulness. Doing so will leave you with nothing but the core function.

For a physical product, subtraction should also be pursued in two other dimensions — weight and size.

Subtract weight

Expense always rises with weight. It is largely through the reduction of weight that living standards rose so markedly during the last century. Economic historians tell us that in the U.S. and UK the weight of all the goods that generated GNP in 2000 was roughly the same as it had been in 1900. Yet that same output was twenty times more valuable in real terms. In other words, products went on a huge diet during the last century — the same value was generated for one-twentieth the weight.[5] A typical timepiece bought in 1900 would have been a heavy fob watch. Contrast that with a Swatch. The latter is far more accurate yet weighs much less, and costs a fraction of its predecessor. Even money itself is lighter. Contrast a 1900 gold sovereign with today's paper money, a credit card, or especially an electronic bank transfer.

Products also lost weight when manufacturers started using lighter versions of existing materials (such as Ford's vanadium steel), when they developed entirely new materials (such as plastics), when they eliminated heavy components, and when they replaced hardware with software.

Follow Henry Ford's advice:

"Start with an article that suits and then ... find some way of eliminating the entirely useless parts. This applies to everything — a shoe, a dress, a house, a piece of machinery, a railroad, a steamship, an airplane. As we cut out the useless parts and simplify necessary ones we also cut down the cost of making. This is simple logic, but oddly enough the ordinary process starts with a cheapening of the manufacturing instead of with a simplifying of the article. The start ought to be with the article. First we ought to find whether it is as well made as it should be — does it give the best possible service? Then — are the materials the best or merely the most expensive? Then — can its complexity and weight be cut down ... A great deal of poverty grows out of the carriage of excess weight."[6]

Ford aimed to make his cars as light as possible, which would lower the cost of making them, lower the cost of running them and increase their reliability:

"With the Ford, there are only 7.95 pounds to be carried by each cubic inch of piston displacement. This is ... why Ford cars are "always going" wherever you see them — through sand and mud, through slush, snow, and water, up hills, across fields and roadless plains ... The more a motor car weighs, the more fuel and lubricants are used.[7]

Someday, we shall discover how further to eliminate weight. Take wood, for example. For certain purposes wood is now the best substance we know, but wood is extremely wasteful. The wood in a Ford car contains thirty pounds of water. There must be a way of doing better than that."[8]

Subtract size

Expense also increases with size. A bigger product uses more materials, and it occupies more space throughout its journey from assembly to the consumer's hands — more space in the factory, the warehouse, the shop, and during transportation between these stages and finally to the consumer. It is no accident that those products that have slimmed down most over the past decades have also been those that have seen the greatest price reductions and consequent explosions in demand: computers, mobile phones, music players, and other electronic devices, and, of course, the biggest space-saver of all — the Cloud. Investigate every possible means of miniaturizing the product, and of saving space, especially in transit. (Recall Ingvar Kamprad's table legs and those IKEA mugs.)

Step Two: Reduce Variety — Invent a Universal Product

Successful simplifiers slash the variety of what is offered to customers in order to cut costs and prices. Ideally, a single "universal product" emerges, one that is both cheaper to produce and achieves high fame and scale: the Model T Ford; the Big Mac; IKEA's light-colored pine furniture; Penguin books; the Honda Supercub; single-class travel on Southwest Airlines.

Consolidating many different products into a few — or just one — has really strong economic advantages: large reduction in stock-keeping units; higher stock turns; lower purchasing costs with greater volume per product; lower marketing and selling costs; and lower production costs. Moreover, a universal product stands out from the crowd as an anomaly, so it attracts attention and commands respect, reducing the need for advertising and the cost of international growth, and multiplying visibility and sales.

In redesigning your product, ask yourself, "Can I invent a

universal product, or something close to it, that incurs much lower costs and has the potential to appeal throughout the world?" Price-simplifiers invariably think like this. Recall Ray Kroc, who wanted to make McDonald's burgers and fries identical in appearance and taste everywhere. Simplicity breeds universality; and universality demands simplicity.

Many "information" products — such as Dropbox, Google, and Spotify — have used the internet to become universal products with remarkable speed by focusing on a single element of utility: I want to broadcast or narrowcast a headline (Twitter); I want to text messages privately (Snapchat); I want to know who is attractive, nearby, and interested in me (Tinder). Speed and ease of communication are complemented by the weightlessness of software from a production point of view, and the ability to give the product away for free (mass distribution) in order to lure in premium (paying) customers or to create a large and valuable audience. Also, and increasingly, when people choose a communication standard the network effects create a scalable business model that can generate a global brand seemingly overnight.

Step Three: Add Cheap Benefits

The third step is to provide benefits that cost the price-simplifier little but have substantial value for target customers. Often these benefits can cost the simplifying firm nothing whatsoever — or even less than nothing when the additional volume of customers and their spending are taken in account.

Earlier, we saw several cases of price-simplifiers offering customers inexpensive extra features — for instance, IKEA's free parking lots, childcare, and restaurants — in compensation for eliminating expensive features, such as pre-assembled furniture and home delivery. This might seem like a simple case of boosting the balance sheet by withdrawing expensive features and replacing them with cheap ones, but in fact it is far better than that for IKEA. All of the firm's apparent "gifts" increase profits *in themselves*, usually by attracting more trade. Anything that generates more volume has high marginal value, and this usually more than offsets the extra cost of providing the service. But beware of complicating the product or business system, and avoid anything that might raise the price.

If you can, conduct a controlled experiment — at different times and/or in different places — to see whether your basic offering, or something additional, generates more net profits.

Once your product has been redesigned, it's time to consider how to redesign the business system around it, how to deliver your simplified product to customers in a way that makes the whole industry vastly more efficient, and shuts out rival firms. This is an even more ambitious and critical task because you are aiming to do nothing less than transform your industry. We explain how you might go about that in the next chapter.

How to Price-Simplify

Part II: Business System Redesign
and Scale Up

True prosperity is marked by a reduction of prices.[1]

Henry Ford

As we saw in Chapter 9, proposition-simplifying begins and ends with redesigning the product. We have also seen that product redesign is crucial when price-simplifying. But the price-simplifier has an even more fascinating and far-reaching mission than that. Once the product has been simplified, they must set about rejigging their entire business system and creating a new mass market.

In Chapter 10 we described the first three steps to becoming a price-simplifier, all of which related to product redesign. But price-simplifiers need to go further than this by transforming their total business system and ensuring that it is scaled up to become dominant and irreplaceable. Let us remind ourselves of the nine steps in the overall process.

We have already described Steps One to Three in Chapter 10. Now let's look at the rest.

Redesign the Business System to Transform Your Industry

There are five steps you can take to redesign your business system:

- Step Four — Automate;
- Step Five — Orchestrate;
- Step Six — Co-opt customers;
- Step Seven — Sell direct; and
- Step Eight — Use simpler technology.

It is unusual for any business system redesign to take all five of these steps. Typically, one step is pre-eminently important while a couple of others are significant as well. You may skip a step entirely if it isn't relevant to your business, provided that you settle on one or two that have the potential to turn your industry upside down. Having said that, in most of our case studies, the next two steps (Four and Five) have proved vital.

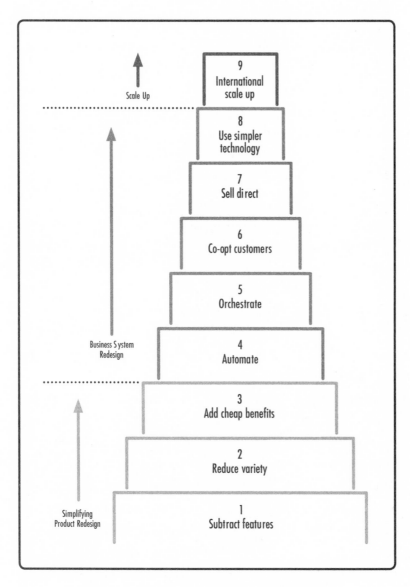

Figure 5: Nine steps to becoming a price-simplifier

Step Four: Automate

By "automate," we mean that you should standardize a product or service so that it can be repeated more automatically, with the result that it demands fewer resources and/ or less managerial intervention, and enables you to operate at much greater scale while maintaining consistent quality. The common theme is a dramatic reduction in cost. But automation can take many different forms, and the payoff is greatest when an entrepreneur automates something that has previously been regarded as "impossible" to automate. For example, the moving assembly line made it possible to automate the production of cars; the Betfair betting exchange automated placing a bet; Tinder automated finding a sexual partner; and the Uber app automated ordering a taxi. Paradoxically, automating a market and a business system can be an highly creative process, and entrepreneurs who have succeeded in doing it say that it is extremely gratifying intellectually (as well as financially).

To see how it can be done, let's think about how Henry Ford automated car production, because this is still one of the best examples for any price-simplifier to follow. "His hallmark was eclecticism," says the historian Richard Tedlow.[2] Ford had to experiment, because nobody had built cars in such volumes before — there was no model of mass production to follow in automobiles or indeed in any comparable industry.[3]

Ford started with product redesign — the Model T was the ninth car model he produced, and it took him five years to get it right. We've already described how he designed the Model T to make it robust yet cheap, but we haven't mentioned that he designed it in such a way that its production could be *automated*. In 1903, five years before the Model T, Ford told one of his partners, "The way to make automobiles is to make one automobile like another automobile, to make them all alike, to make them come from the factory just alike — just like one pin is like another pin when it comes from a pin factory."[4]

He started with a price target of $600, found initially (in 1909) that the lowest he could price his car was $950, but then experimented to reach his goal. There were four milestones in Ford's quest for automation. First, he built the biggest factory in the world at Highland Park, which opened on New Year's Day, 1910. Second, he organized production so that employees moved from one work station to another in a prescribed order. This, and the advantages of scale, decreased the cost of the Model T to the $600 price target by 1912. But Ford was still not satisfied. His third milestone was, as he put it, to "take the work to the man rather than the man to the work"[5]. By concocting a series of conveyor belts, rollways and gravity slides, the manufacture of everything except the chassis (the final stage) was put on to a moving line in 1913. The production line had arrived, replacing batch production. As a result, the price of the car was cut again, to $550. The fourth and final step was when Ford put the assembly of the chassis on to a moving line as well. Prior to this, it took 12 hours and 28 minutes to assemble each chassis; by the spring of 1914, the assembly line had cut this to just 1 hour and 33 minutes. The price of the Model T fell to $490 in 1914, and $360 in 1916.

Three and a half decades later, the McDonald brothers had the brilliant idea to adapt Ford's moving assembly line to the production of hamburgers and fries. Previously, nobody had thought of using a production-line system in a service industry. Once again, standardization and process design were spectacularly successful. Once again, automation was only possible because product variety was severely curtailed and the product was totally standardized — one hamburger was exactly the same as another. By 1993, McDonald's had sold one hundred billion of those identical hamburgers.

Budget airlines, while not automating in the traditional sense, simplified the product and redesigned the process to produce a more standardized product with fewer moving parts, fewer choices and decisions, and therefore much lower costs than their full-service rivals. The process flows of budget airlines are machine-like — higher repetition, less variation, fewer exceptions. By contrast, traditional airlines used an ever-expanding, ever more complex, hub-and-spoke system that made cost control impossible. It is much harder to automate a service with several travel classes, high variation in operating policies, and a huge number of destinations.

You can simplify almost anything if you view it as a product to be standardized and automated as far as is humanly possible. If air travel and restaurants can be automated, and a mass market created by offering very low prices, the same must be true for any other sector.

Opportunity lies wherever an industry has not yet been automated.

Step Five: Orchestrate

IKEA is a prime example of how to orchestrate. Orchestration means pulling the strings in an industry by seizing the high ground — the customers — and then co-opting independent players into your new system. They benefit, but you benefit even more.

Before IKEA, you had furniture-makers, most of whom were small scale. You also had retailers, again mostly small scale. You had customers, most of whom were confused as to where to go to buy what they wanted, and often daunted by the high prices of decent furniture. And you had logistics providers — transport companies that were mainly firms outside the industry, for whom furniture was a minor product. No strong brands. No integration. No economic logic. High prices, but generally low profits.

IKEA provided a unifying plan — to the great benefit of customers. And IKEA itself.

The business system is close to perfect, because:

- It achieves stunning economic benefits for customers, who are happy to play their part in the orchestra.
- The combination of retail scale and design/brand power renders manufacturers subservient.
- Once the system was fully in place, there was no room for a larger imitator. The IKEA system could have been imitated in a particular national market, but without IKEA's overall scale any imitator would have been hamstrung by much higher costs and prices. As with any successful business system, scale feeds its power, providing protection against all comers.

Dell Computer was another successful orchestrator when it became the most successful supplier of PCs in the 1990s, taking market leadership from Compaq in 1999 and holding that lead through to 2004. Michael Dell's business model combined orchestration with direct selling. It involved:

- Scouring Asia for the lowest-cost computer manufacturers, then controlling and orchestrating those companies, without making any financial investment in them.
- Selling direct to firms and individuals, initially by phone and from 1996 through Dell's dedicated website. This shredded costs and gave Dell a large competitive advantage. In 1999, Compaq, having lost market share to its lower-priced rival, started to sell direct over the internet too, but its retailers forced the firm to abandon this strategy.
- Offering customers the ability to personalize their computers by allowing an almost infinite number of permutations: customers could telephone the factory direct to instruct Dell of their preferences. This may appear to contradict our advice to standardize and eliminate variety as much as possible, but every rule has an exception. Dell found a low-cost way to personalize machines by working to order and thus avoiding the most dangerous cost of variety — that of unsold stock.
- Operating on short cycle times, with reduced inventory. Holding inventory is a large cost penalty in the PC industry, where new machines cost less than old ones.
- Having the lowest operating costs in the industry. Dell's operating costs in 2002 were 10 percent of its revenues. Those of its main rivals, Compaq and Gateway, were more than double that. In addition, Dell was able to expand without the need to source extra funds

because it operated on negative working capital, receiving money from customers before it paid its suppliers.

Dell's prices were much lower and its net margins significantly higher than those of its competitors. The formula worked until around 2005, when Dell attempted to move upmarket and started to manufacture several products that did not fit within its price-simplifying formula.

The same dynamic is evident in two of the most successful industry orchestrators today — Walmart and Amazon — both of which ruthlessly exploit the benefits of scale, brand and, most importantly, a strong customer relationship with a significant proportion of the U.S. population. Because these two orchestrators enjoy such enormous customer volumes, they are able to force their suppliers to cut their prices to the bone; and because their prices are so low, they are able to maintain enormous customer volumes.

Step Six: Co-opt Customers

IKEA's business system has three strings to its bow: the main string, which is orchestration; and two secondary strings — automation and co-opting customers. IKEA's method of co-option is similar to that employed by McDonald's and the budget airlines. There is an implicit deal with the customers — they take on some of the functions that used to be performed by the firm, and in exchange the firm cuts prices down to levels that the customers can afford.

As we've said before, with IKEA, the customer assumes the job of final assembly — a huge part of the total old system cost. The customer also effectively takes on the traditional role of the salesperson by using a catalog and following signs to find the product they want. They then carry their goods to the checkout and take them home — jobs that in the old system required expensive warehouses and a fleet of delivery trucks.

In McDonald's, the customer takes on the job of the waiting staff, some of the kitchen staff and even some of the cleaners. By participating in this system, the customers enjoy lower prices and faster service than they would in a traditional restaurant; and McDonald's benefits because it greatly reduces its labor costs. Moreover, because customers are prepared to accept a short menu, McDonald's can buy its ingredients in bulk, lowering its costs and prices still further.

When traveling on a budget airline, the customers facilitate greater speed of boarding and punctuality by accepting that they will have to queue and fit into a tight schedule. They buy their tickets and check in online, doing the job that travel agents used to do. They sometimes carry their own bags — which are strictly limited in size and weight — on and off the plane, making baggage handlers unnecessary. They also pay for their food and drink, and accept that they will probably have less space and legroom than on a scheduled flight.

When added together, these compromises make a large economic difference. The customer cheerfully accepts them because the end result is an unbeatably low price for the airline's principal function — getting passengers from A to B. Sometimes it seems that the passengers are serving the airline rather than the other way round, but this is the modern way of doing business, and it makes perfect economic sense for both parties. Again, it explains why low prices can coexist with unprecedented rates of growth and profit for the budget airlines.

Firms that co-opt customers are really orchestrating them. Like all forms of orchestration, the benefits of vertical integration are enjoyed without the cost of ownership. For example, IKEA's customers are the equivalent of an in-house delivery service. The orchestrator is like a benign spider, welcoming suppliers and customers into its web, with the main technique being seduction. Suppliers are seduced by high volumes. Customers are seduced by rock-bottom prices. The market is redefined because the suppliers and customers complement each other, and both gravitate to the common space demarcated by the orchestrator.

Such transactions can be found in exchanges or electronic marketplaces, such as eBay, the New York Stock Exchange and Uber, as well as on hundreds of other sites that are proliferating by the day. Buyers and sellers are autonomous individuals, not owned in any way by the marketplace. But each is greatly attracted by the other's presence in the orchestrator's system.

Step Seven: Sell Direct

Direct selling is not new. It grows in fits and starts, responding to changes in technology.

In the early nineteenth century there were no chain stores selling general merchandise. But with the advent of the railways it became possible to ship goods across countries, even one as vast as the United States. First to take advantage of this new transport system to sell goods by mail-order catalog was Aaron Montgomery Ward in 1874. The following decade, the great publicist and salesman Richard W. Sears — who could, according to Henry Goldman (of Goldman Sachs), "sell a breath of fresh air"[6] — entered the industry. But he went further, because his firm — Sears, Roebuck — was willing to accept cash on delivery and offer a money-back guarantee. By providing a better deal than Montgomery Ward, and undercutting retail stores by about a quarter, Sears had become the market leader by 1900.

Sears' new business system was based on offering the widest range of goods, making the largest purchases of items from producers large and small, and the company's extraordinary catalog, with lyrical copy originally written by Sears himself. When asked which American book he would give to every Russian if he had the chance, Franklin D. Roosevelt allegedly replied, "The Sears catalog."

As Richard Tedlow says:

"Sears was about 'the humbling of the products.' Some products may have been available only in certain areas, but Sears brought them everywhere. Other products may have been technically complex or expensive machines, previously sold only to the elite. Sears pushed the price down and sold them to the average citizen."[7]

Just as every new generation believes it has invented sex, so, with a little more justification, every generation believes it has invented direct selling. With new technologies come new kinds of direct selling — from the postal service to the phone, the fax (remember the fax?), email (still one of the best media if used selectively with Sears-like attention to copy quality) and the ultimate (to date), in terms of simplicity, convenience and low cost, the internet, including the new ways of selling through Facebook, Google, eBay, and other social media.

But a word of caution: each new generation of direct selling does not necessarily — or even usually — result in a price revolution. For that to happen, two conditions must be met: any price reduction must be real and significant; and the business system must be original and sufficiently defensible to repel effective competition. This is rare.

Price-simplifying through direct selling kicks in when at least two of the following three conditions apply:

- An expensive middleman is eliminated.
- New technology is used in some shape or form.
- There is a clever simplifying idea at the root of the new business.

Let's work through this idea with the help of three case studies.

Direct Line

Started by three British entrepreneurs in 1985, Direct Line transformed the motor insurance business. First, it cut out the insurance brokers who stood between the underwriters — the syndicates who actually insure the risk — and the motorists. That saved about 20 percent. This was a good start, but not enough.

The founders realized that the motor insurance market "average-priced" the cost of insurance. Because it was widely believed that it was impossible to predict the likelihood of an individual car owner having a crash, everyone was charged pretty much the same. But what if you *knew* that Mrs. Jones was far less likely than Mr. Black to be involved in a crash? If you could target the 20 percent of drivers who were least likely to have an accident, you could afford to cut their premiums in half and still make a tidy profit.

So was it possible to discriminate in this way? Yes, it was, as long as you used the telephone (and later the internet) to offer direct quotes to individuals. This was the "direct" part of Direct Line, and it had the added benefit of costing the firm less than the traditional system.

But how was Direct Line able to predict who would probably be a safe driver in the future? This was where technological advances were crucial. In the 1960s and 1970s, only a powerful mainframe computer, costing around £2 million, would have been able to do the necessary analysis. But with the advent of personal computers in the early 1980s it was suddenly possible to buy a second-hand mainframe for around £20,000. Direct Line invested in several of them and set about creating a database that estimated the probability of any specific individual — defined by several demographic indicators — claiming on their car insurance. Once the system was up and running a caller would receive their quote in seconds, and if the database declared that they were a good risk the premium would be much lower than any they had received elsewhere. So, for the right customers, the new system was dramatically cheaper, as well as faster and more convenient.

Despite competitors imitating Direct Line, the strength of its brand and its matchless reputation for offering the lowest prices has enabled it to remain the UK's market leader for more than a quarter of a century. It also now operates in Spain, Germany, Italy, and Japan.

Charles Schwab & Co

In 1975 Charles Schwab & Co became the world's first discount broker, cutting commission rates by 80 percent. In 1982 it became the first broker to offer a 24/7 order entry and quote service. By 2011, the company had 8.2 million brokerage customers, with $1.65 trillion in assets.[8] At the time of writing, the firm is valued at $39.3 billion.

Schwab automated the brokering process, eliminating the client's individual stockbroker–adviser, subtracting the "advice" part of the service, and using new technology to enable clients to enter the stock market directly. Eventually, through product redesign, automation, intelligent use of the internet and huge scale, Schwab managed to cut costs and prices to less than a tenth of their original level.

The Vanguard Group

Financier John Bogle started the first index tracker fund on 31 December 1975. His Vanguard Group cut out the role of the active fund manager, instead investing simply in a "basket" of shares from the stock market index. The index fund idea rested on three decades' worth of academic work which indicated that fund managers, in aggregate, underperformed stock market indices. This explosive finding — that an enormously well-paid industry was both parasitic and unnecessary — was fascinating, but nobody had done anything about it before Bogle.

His index fund cut annual fees by up to 90 percent — a great example of price-simplifying. It was ridiculed at the time as "Bogle's folly," with the chairman of Fidelity Investments declaring that he couldn't "believe that the great mass of investors are going to be satisfied with receiving just average returns." Vanguard is now the largest mutual fund in the United States, with $3.0 trillion under management.[9] It has since been emulated by numerous imitators, yet it still claims to have 10 percent of all available global investment funds.[10]

Can you think of a new way to sell direct, using new technology that nobody has yet applied to your industry?

Step Eight: Use Simpler Technology

One of the best business books of the last twenty years is *The Innovator's Dilemma* by Harvard professor Clayton Christensen. He documents how new, technically inferior, yet much cheaper technology — what he calls *disruptive* technology — changes markets and usually results in a new market leader.[11] "Products based on disruptive technologies," Christensen says, "are typically cheaper, simpler, smaller, and, frequently, more convenient to use."[12] His examples include transistors' disruption of vacuum tubes (and semiconductors' subsequent disruption of transistors), steel mini-mills' disruption of integrated steel-makers, cable-actuated excavators losing out to hydraulic excavators, and small disk drives replacing larger ones. More recent examples (which do not feature in Christensen's 1997 book) include computer tablets and smartphones disrupting the laptop market, and apps such as Uber and Airbnb challenging the traditional taxi and cheaper hotels markets. (Indeed, *all* apps have the potential to disrupt their respective industries, though the great majority fail to do so.)

The story typically plays out in the following way. First, the new technology satisfies only the bottom end of the market. For example, steel mini-mills, which are less than a tenth the size of a traditional integrated mill, began operating in the late 1960s, but initially the steel they produced, though much cheaper, was good enough for only the lowest-grade application — steel reinforcing bars.

Second, big companies, although they have the option to use the new technology, shun it. They tend to do this for several apparently very good reasons. One is that big companies' customers usually say that they are not interested in the new technology and its cheaper products because their performance is inadequate for their needs. Another is that "it is very difficult for a company whose cost structure is tailored to compete in high-end markets to be profitable in low-end markets as well" — established companies are used to operating with high overheads. Finally, "small markets don't solve the growth needs of large companies"[13] and "markets that don't exist can't be analyzed."[14] These are all powerful arguments *against* the adoption of many new technologies. In the case of mini-mills, no major integrated steel-maker anywhere in the world chose to make the transition.

Third, since the established market leaders fail to embrace the new technology, it falls to generally small-scale recent entrants to the industry to champion the new products and try to find a market for them through trial and error; typically, at first, in new applications. For instance, Nucor and Chaparral began at the bottom of the steel market — bars and rods — before gradually moving up to more demanding applications, such as structural steel, and finally to high-level sheet steel. This is the typical pattern: the new technology improves its performance until it ultimately satisfies most or all of the main market. Moreover, the old technology usually improves at the same time, but to such an extent that it eventually outstrips the requirements of almost every customer. It becomes unnecessary to use the old technology because the new, simpler products are more than adequate. As Christensen says, "when the performance of two or more competing products has improved beyond what the market demands ... the basis of product choice evolves from functionality to reliability, then to convenience, and, ultimately, to price."[15]

Enter the price-simplifier. One of the newcomers to the industry tends to win by being in the right place at the right time, adopting the new technology, providing the lowest-cost and price product, and scaling up to take the leading market position.

When Christensen's book was published, the leading mini-mill company, F. Kenneth Iverson's Nucor, accounted for just 7 percent of the North American sheet-steel market, which, as he says, was "hardly enough to concern the integrated mills, because Nucor's success has been limited to the commoditized, least-profitable end of their product line'. But Christensen boldly forecast that Nucor would soon challenge and ultimately overtake the integrated steel-makers, such as Bethlehem and U.S.X, which were then riding high on the stock market:

"[T]he integrated steel companies' march to the profitable northeast [high-specification] corner of the steel industry is a story of aggressive investment, rational decision making, close attention to the needs of mainstream customers, and record profits. It is the same innovator's dilemma that confounded the leading providers of disk drives and mechanical excavators: Sound managerial decisions are at the very root of their impending fall from industry leadership."[16]

Christensen was proved right. Nucor, a small and marginally profitable company in 1996, is now the market leader in the U.S. steel market and a Fortune 300 company.

So, if there is a new, inferior but much cheaper technology that has not yet been seriously adopted in your industry, and if it has the potential to cut costs in half, you would be wise to jump in before anyone else does. Construct a business system around it so that you can become — and remain — *the* low-price player.

Scale Up

Step Nine: Scale Up and Roll Out Internationally

Your firm will be most vulnerable when you have redesigned the product and the business system and have just started to put them in place. If the price cut is significant, if the design is good and you have developed a universal product, and if the business system is unique, simple, and elegant, you will win ... *unless another firm copies your approach and builds volume faster than you do.* If that happens, you will almost certainly lose.

Scaling up quickly is therefore vital. Maximize sales and take an early lead, even if that means operating at zero or negative margins for a few years. If cash is a constraint, seek venture capital. As volumes build, your costs will decline and you will be able to take a small margin on high revenues.

Once the concept is proven in one place, take it nation-wide, then international and global as quickly as possible. History shows that when a firm with a genuinely universal and attractive product — such as Coca-Cola or eBay — leaves a gap in a market, allowing a local imitator to grab first-mover advantage, they may never recover. For instance, Coke was slow to enter the Middle East and, as a result, Pepsi took the lead there, a lead it has never sur-rendered. eBay was similarly sluggish in Eastern Europe. When it finally arrived, a dominant business — Allegro — was already in its way, and it is now one of the largest e-commerce players in the region.

Conclusion

Price-simplifying offers the prospect of building huge vol-umes — admittedly, at low margins, but with huge growth in revenues and profits for decades to come. The ultimate prize — if you do everything right and build a unique business system that is too large to be replicated, and if you continue to cut costs and prices and increase international volume — is long-term market leadership.

But what about *current* market leaders? Should they sim-plify? If so, when. And how? And what are the dangers if they don't?

Key Points for Chapters 10 and 11

1. To cut prices in half, you need to redesign and simplify your product from first principles. Subtract features. Reduce variety. Create a universal product.

2. You must also redesign your business system to build a simple, proprietary system that lets you deliver stunningly low prices that your rivals cannot match.

3. Your best defense against imitation is to scale up so quickly and extensively that no nooks or crannies are left in which a rival can take root. Nowadays this requires early, preferably immediate, international rollout — whatever it costs and however hard it might seem to achieve.

PART THREE

Save the Dinosaurs?

In Part Three we switch the perspective from that of the poacher to that of the gamekeeper. How can market leaders who are not simplifiers protect themselves from actual or potential insurgents? How serious are the threats to non-simplifying leading companies? Why do they often shun the opportunity to simplify when it is perfectly feasible — and usually not too expensive — for them to take the plunge? Finally, if they do decide to protect themselves, which of the several approaches available to them is most likely to succeed?

12

Do They Need Saving?

Long runs on Broadway are rare.

Tom Peters

A re market leaders naturally vulnerable to simplifiers? What are the warning signs?

Can we conclude from our research that market leaders are typically vulnerable when faced with firms that start to simplify their markets?

The honest answer is: *we don't know.*

On the one hand, a long and impressive roll-call of blue-chip firms have seen their market value and profits collapse almost overnight when challenged by simplifying insurgents. For instance:

- In the 1960s, IBM lost a large portion of its market when

DEC introduced "minicomputers," which, as the name suggests, were much smaller and simpler than mainframes. (Although minicomputers themselves were huge and complex by today's standards.)

- Two decades later, despite being the PC market leader from 1981 to 1985, IBM again suffered at the hands of simplifiers, outflanked by the price-simplifiers Compaq, Hewlett-Packard, and Dell, and unable to stop proposition-simplifier Apple securing the lucrative upper tier of the market. IBM finally stopped making computers in 2005.

- DEC and Wang also lost their businesses to the PC price-simplifiers in the 1980s, having been the dominant forces in their respective segments — minicomputers and word processors.

- Xerox succumbed to Canon and Ricoh after the insurgents introduced smaller, simpler copiers that could sit on a manager's desk.

- Integrated steel mills, such as Bethlehem and U.S.X, lost market leadership to price simplifier Nucor with its lower-cost mini-mills.

- Pan-Am, TWA, and American Airlines all filed for bankruptcy after losing U.S. market leadership to Southwest Airlines.

- Kodak lost out to Sony when the latter introduced digital cameras.

- Lotus, once the world's leading software firm, fell to price-simplifier Microsoft.

- Encyclopaedia Britannica, which had been the market leader for 222 years, was wiped out by price-simplifiers Encarta and Wikipedia.

- Nokia, once the dominant mobile phone manufacturer, was devastated by Apple's and Samsung's introduction of smartphones.
- The video-rental market leader, Blockbuster, was outgunned by Netflix.
- AltaVista lost its lead in online searching to Google.
- Barnes & Noble was humbled by Amazon.
- Then came dozens of other examples of digital companies ousting their real-world counterparts. In all these cases market leadership was forfeited to a simpler and cheaper provider, or to a proposition-simplifier whose product was a joy to use.

In light of this list, it would be easy to argue that simplifying firms with clearly superior propositions and/or simpler business models typically win ... as long as the change they initiate is sufficiently radical.

The problem with this argument, however, is that it is statistically weak. There are just not enough examples to generalize. There is also the issue of survivor bias: we don't celebrate — and rarely even recall — when a leading firm sees off the challenge of a simplifying rival.

For sure, there is a general tendency for simplifiers to emerge victorious, but it is not inevitable. There are plenty of counter-examples, such as the hotel industry, which has quite complex international systems, yet nobody has come close to challenging Hilton or Marriott. Airbnb — valued at $10 billion in a private equity transaction in April 2014 — may triple the size of the bed-and-breakfast industry, eat into the lower and middle reaches of the hotel sector, and, as it owns no hotels itself, become extremely profitable, but it is no threat to the luxury hotels. They will only succumb to a "joy to stay" innovator, and it is hard to see that happening … yet. At present, the big boys' rivals are mainly local boutique hotels that are able to trade on their unique locations and the individual skills of their owner–managers, so they cannot be replicated on a large scale.

There is also the food industry, where giants such as General Mills and Kellogg's do not appear to be vulnerable to simplifying rivals. Similarly, the hugely complex firms of Unilever and Procter & Gamble have faced no serious challengers. Their brands — many of which are several decades old — seem to insulate them from competition. How long this situation will last is a matter of conjecture, not statistics.

Furthermore, simplifiers do not always face a single dominant player. Sometimes the dinosaurs form a large pack of similar-sized animals. McDonald's, Direct Line, Starbucks, Twitter, IKEA, and many other simplifiers transformed their industries without replacing a dominant leader, because there wasn't one when they began. These simplifiers did not kill Goliath; they drove dozens of smaller operators out of business.

Warning Signals Tests

Certainly, dominant firms cannot afford to be complacent. The sensible approach is to watch out for the wrecking ball, and take steps to avoid it before it is too late. The attacks can come from price-simplifiers and/or from proposition-simplifiers. Their respective warning signals are somewhat different from each other.

Warning Signals from Price-Simplifiers

1. A much cheaper product emerges. It does not matter if the new product's performance is inferior. If it is *good enough* for the market, it is a serious threat. The mere existence of a product that is 25–50 percent cheaper should set off alarm bells for the leader. The only safe assumption to make is that the new product will gain in performance and become even cheaper as volume increases and its business system develops. It also does not matter if the new product is rejected by your customers and attracts only a new type of customer. Your customers may change their minds later, once the product improves and becomes even less expensive.

2. The firms making the new product are recently established. This means that their impact cannot be determined as yet and that they may not be constrained by traditional ways of operating.

3. The new entrants are playing the game differently. Their product may be smaller, lighter, faster, or all three. It may be based on new technology. It may be based on customers accepting some of the work that is performed for them in the established system. The business system itself may be different. The challengers may be more specialized, making only one product or a few, so their product range is far narrower than those of established firms.

4. At least one simplifying firm is growing fast. Even if it has a tiny market share at present, it may soon start to grow exponentially. This is easy to overlook or

underestimate. Do not rely on market statistics; investigate the firm's potential growth directly.

5. The new firm has lower margins than yours. Its business may seem to be unprofitable, or only marginally profitable. This is a warning because it may discourage you from making the new product yourself.

6. The new product has the potential to cost much less to make than your rival product. If the new firm were to achieve your volumes, would it be able to undercut you by 50 percent or more?

7. Your firm could make the new product but chooses not to. If you want to make a new product, you will find a way to do it. If you decide not to make it, your decision will be hard to rescind, even when the product becomes viable.

Warning Signals from Proposition-Simplifiers

You will notice that the first three warnings here are different from those in the previous list:

1. The product or service is designed differently. It is radically simpler, using a new method or technology, or it is based on different assumptions about what is important to the customer.

2. The new product is a joy to use.

3. The product is priced at a premium to yours, yet it is eating into your market share.

4. The challenger is playing the game differently.

5. The firm or firms are recent entrants to the market.

6. At least one of the new entrants is growing fast.

7. Your firm either can't make the new product or chooses
   not to.

For more insights into how you can spot price- or proposition-simplifying in your market, and for support in
formulating your response, visit www.SIMPLIFYforCEOs.
com.

Key Points

1. There is no inevitability about the decline of market
   leaders. Simplifying firms' threat to them may never
   materialize.
2. But it may do. There are numerous examples of hugely
   successful and dominant firms losing out to challengers that originally seemed puny. The Warning Signal
   Tests should be taken now and at frequent intervals.
3. It is prudent to make contingency plans for what to do
   if you face a simplifier.

It is hard for established firms to deal with a new type of
competition, because managers in successful firms are generally loathe to simplify. In the next chapter, we outline the
threats to market leaders that may emerge from *inside*, rather
than outside, the firm.

13

The Weakness of Strong Firms

Five Bad Reasons Why Managers Don't Simplify

To survive for the long haul, you must passionately pursue the destruction of what you have created. The question: Can you passionately pursue perfection and destruction simultaneously?[1]

Tom Peters

There is plenty of anecdotal evidence that managers in large, successful firms consistently tend to use to make their businesses more complex rather than simpler. But why do they do that?

It turns out that there are five reasons why managers in market leaders don't simplify, and they are all traps. We call them: the Overhead Trap; the Cannibalization Trap; the Customer Trap; the Complexity Trap; and the Skills Trap.

Nearly always, market leaders *could* simplify; it's just that they choose not to. Those whom the gods wish to destroy they first make complex.

The Overhead Trap

When I (Richard) co-founded the strategy consulting firm LEK in 1983, we entered a joint venture with a much larger and more established firm, PA Consulting. PA had practices devoted to management consulting, human resources, telecoms and technology. On several occasions it had also tried to break into LEK's field, the strategy market (a market we shared with BCG, Bain and McKinsey), but it had always failed to make much headway. This wasn't because PA's clients wouldn't buy strategy from them. Rather, PA had never been willing to pay enough money to attract first-rate strategists. The idea of paying any individual several hundred thousand pounds a year was taboo; *nobody* at PA received a six-figure salary in those days.

Then Peter Lawson at PA had the bright idea of instigating the joint venture between his firm and LEK. It operated as PA Strategy Partners: PA provided us with leads and we sold a lot of strategy. There was no organizational problem for PA as they didn't have to pay any of LEK's overheads yet still took a share of the profits. Making a million pounds profit per partner in a separate venture was just fine for them.

It is sometimes observed, correctly, that organizations like to go upmarket, towards higher gross-margin products and customers. Yet making overhead commitments well beyond the norm in an organization can be just as problematic as accepting margins that are much lower. PA was unwilling to add higher-cost expert consultants ahead of demand, even though margins in the strategy business were much higher than those in its core sectors. This lack of comfort with high overheads explains why PA had not previously made any progress in the classic strategy arena.

The other side of the coin — companies' reluctance to accept lower-margin business — has been well documented by earlier studies, so it need not detain us long. Clayton Christensen tells the story of the Micropolis Corporation, founded by Stuart Mabon to make 8-inch disk drives for the computer industry. His firm soon became the leader in that market. Then, when 5.25-inch drives came out, Mabon realized that the new, cheaper disks were a serious threat to his business, so he put his best engineers to work on a project to make them. However, because the 5.25-inch disks were lower margin, his managers kept trying to move the talent back to work on the old 8-inch disks, where Micropolis made most of its money. Although he was the boss, Mabon had to fight a constant rear-guard action to keep his top people working on the new disks. It was, he said, the most exhausting experience of his life, demanding "100 percent of my time and energy for 18 months".[2] Even so, Micropolis never became the market leader in 5.25-inch disks, and before long the market was moving on to even smaller disk drives anyway.

A final example of the Overhead Trap is DEC's failure to make its mark in personal computers. From 1965, when the company introduced the first "minicomputer," until the 1980s, DEC was one of Wall Street's biggest success stories. It was the dominant force in minicomputers, leaving IBM trailing in its wake. But when the PC market began to sprout in the 1970s, DEC looked into entering the new sector *eleven times* and held back every time. It finally started to make PCs only in 1983, two years after IBM and *seven* years after Apple. None of its PC products was ever successful.

Why was that? DEC certainly had the design and technical skills. But the firm was used to a market with different economics. Minicomputers required a huge, ongoing research effort . . . and rewarded it with gross margins north of 50 percent. By contrast, PC gross margins were under 30 percent. Also, the new breed of computers did not require the massive, continuous research investment that minicomputers did, and customers were not willing to pay the sorts of prices that would support expensive research anyway. DEC's belated move into PCs was at the top of that market, where gross margins were highest but volumes were lowest and customer requirements greatest.

It seems that firms develop their own rules of thumb about acceptable margins and then become addicted to them. So, if simpler, lower-margin products come along, it is hard for any successful company to embrace them and realize that, although the margins are lower, the overheads are too. New entrants with simpler products do not have the handicap of success in more complex, more profitable products, and the overhead and margin assumptions that such success generates.

The Cannibalization Trap

In 2000, Betfair, a new betting company, started in London. Other online bookmakers already existed, but Betfair's business model was different from those of all its rivals, online or offline. Instead of setting the odds itself, Betfair created an electronic market — a betting exchange — where gamblers could offer odds to other gamblers or take the odds posted by other individuals.

I (Richard) invested in Betfair early in 2001, acquiring 10 percent of the firm for £1.5 million, meaning the whole company was valued at just £15 million. However, although the firm was minuscule at the time (at least in comparison with the market leaders), it was growing at a rate of around 50 percent a *month*. Within a couple of years, though still relatively small, it was already beginning to make significant inroads into the main betting market. This was not surprising, given that Betfair charged an average commission of 3 percent, compared with the mainstream bookmakers' "overround" — or gross profit margin — of about 12 percent. Moreover, Betfair charged commission only on winning bets. So it was charging just 1.5 percent on total bets — a price reduction of 87.5 percent!

You can understand the traditional bookies' fear of "cannibalization". They saw no sense in adopting the new system themselves and encouraging their customers to move from the current high-margin way of betting towards a much lower-margin method. This is a common concern of any business faced with a disruptive, lower-cost new entrant to their market. But the bookmakers did not realize that, whatever they did, any price-sensitive gambler who was not a total technophobe would soon be beating a path to Betfair's door. The sensible thing, therefore, would have been for one of the "big three" bookmakers in the UK — Ladbrokes, Corals, or William Hill — either to start their own online betting exchange or, better still, buy Betfair for petty cash (in their terms) and thus eliminate a potentially very serious rival. Yet none of them chose either of these options. For them, Betfair was the enemy — a company to be crushed underfoot — preferably by persuading the government to declare betting exchanges illegal.

When the government refused to play ball, Betfair went on to become, at one stage, the number-one online betting company in the UK, with a market value of £1.3 billion. At the time of writing, this had increased to around £3 billion. Meanwhile, the erstwhile leading bookmakers in the traditional market were all overtaken by a new leader, Paddy Power, which provided a wider range of "fun" bets and cut its margins. If one of the big three had acquired Betfair, and kept it as a separate business, they would likely be the market leader now, instead of an also-ran.

The same pattern — fear of cannibalization preventing leading companies from doing anything positive to halt that cannibalization — has occurred across almost the entire field of internet retailing. The leaders in nearly all of the internet retail categories — such as books (Amazon) and auctions (eBay) — are very different from the "real world" leaders. Despite potential advantages from combining bricks-and-mortar retailing with online retailing in the same category — ranging from bargaining leverage with suppliers to using the customer base, to fulfilment and many other synergies — the real world leaders were initially reluctant to go online for fear of cannibalization. And when they realized their mistake, they did too little, too late. Barnes & Noble, for example, was the world's largest bookseller, but it was May 1997 before it finally launched its website, almost two years after Amazon. Once again, fear of cannibalization had led to greater cannibalization than would otherwise have occurred. Amazon now sells far more books than Barnes & Noble.

However, perhaps the greatest victim of fear of cannibalization — and one of the biggest corporate declines ever — was Xerox. The company's patents for plain paper copying gave it a virtual monopoly in the 1950s and 1960s, which Xerox exploited to the fullest. The typical machine cost about $700 to make and was sold for $3000 or more. But nothing lasts forever. In the late 1960s, Canon began to circumvent Xerox's patents and price-simplified, introducing a small desktop copier for less than a third of the price of Xerox's monster machines.[3] Helped by the Federal Trade Commission, which forced Xerox to license its patents to other firms, Canon soon seized market leadership. By 1979, Xerox's U.S. copier market share had plummeted from 99 percent to just 14 percent.

Consider what we call the *cannibalization paradox*:

- The decision to provide a stripped-down, simpler, and much cheaper product is valid if your customers will use that product. If you think they will, you might as well cannibalize yourself before some other firm does it for you. If you think they will never use the cheaper product, it might *seem* to make no sense to introduce it.

And yet:

- If you truly believe that your customers will never switch, there is no danger of cannibalization, so you might as well make the cheaper product anyway and use the profits to top up those from your existing business.

So, with the important exceptions of luxury and niche markets — where customers are not price-sensitive — it logically follows that:

- There is no circumstance in which it makes sense *not* to introduce a simpler and cheaper product!

But logic and psychology are two very different things. It *might* have been sensible for Xerox to continue to milk its customers and delay the introduction of a simpler and cheaper copier until Canon launched its product, or was getting close to doing so. But then Xerox would have needed to act extremely quickly and decisively to cannibalize itself, which would have required having a small machine already in development. Yet the company did nothing. For sure, a determined CEO acting in the shareholders' interests *could* have pushed through development of a small Xerox machine to fend off Canon, regardless of the inevitable opposition from his powerful sales force. But the real world does not work like that. The fear of cannibalization paralyzes successful management, delaying action until it is too late.

The Customer Trap

Why did it take so long for full-service airlines to imitate their budget rivals, despite the latter's obvious success? The first full-service foray into enemy space was United's Shuttle service, launched in 1994, *twenty-three years* after Southwest Airlines started operating. Perhaps it was fear of cannibalizing the firm's established customers, but we think it was more likely the opposite. The Customer Trap is when you assume that your customers aren't interested in the new business model.

This is usually true ... at first. Southwest appealed to people who wanted to travel point-to-point — those who had previously driven or had not traveled long distances at all. It did not appeal to the sophisticated frequent fliers who traveled to major cities, often abroad, and comprised most of the scheduled airlines' market. But when a mass market is created, the new product gradually becomes increasingly visible. The number of budget airlines grew, and their reach gradually extended, so that *everyone* traveling on a full fare became aware of the much cheaper alternatives. And, ultimately, money always talks. Business people started to use budget airlines when traveling at their own expense, and learned that they were not so bad: they still had a seat (albeit with less legroom) and they arrived safely and usually on time, just as on a scheduled flight. Then, when the economy suffered a downturn, ever more small- and medium-sized firms made their staff use the cheaper carriers for business flights, too; and these habits persisted even when the economy improved.

What happened in the airline market reflects a general pattern. In *The Innovator's Dilemma*, Clayton Christensen documents how, time and again — in the mechanical excavator industry, in motorcycles, in the steel-making and in dozens of other examples — the leading firms' customers initially do not want the new product. When Honda accidentally stumbled across a new market — off-road dirt-biking — for its Supercub in California around 1960, nobody viewed the Japanese firm as much of a threat to the motorbike market leader, Harley-Davidson. Honda's customers were different, and the company sold its bikes through sporting goods shops, not through motorcycle dealerships. Harley's customers wanted *serious* bikes, not puny Japanese toys, no matter how cute they looked. But then, once Honda had secured a toe-hold in the market, it began to develop more powerful bikes that were intended for use on the road. Bit by bit, model by model, the firm moved upmarket, and Harley-Davidson was gradually forced to retreat. After failing to compete effectively with Honda in the 100–300cc range, and later in the 500–750cc range, Harley repositioned itself solely at the high end of the market. Although high margin, this sector was much smaller than the others, and Harley fell on hard times. It has managed to rationalize itself as a successful premium brand today, boosted by a successful clothing side-business, but Honda sells three times as many motorcycles worldwide.

The trap here is that the market leader believes its customers, and so ignores the threat from the new product. The typical pattern can be summarized as follows:

- The performance of the new product gradually improves, and after a while it meets the requirements of all but the most demanding customers.
- With increased learning and volume, the simpler product becomes ever cheaper, which makes the price difference between it and the premium product increasingly hard to ignore.

As this happens, the typical response of the market leader — such as Harley — is "segment retreat" — a move to even more complex and expensive products. This is usually explained as a natural response to short-term earnings pressure from the simpler product. Such an explanation is often valid, but something else may also be involved . . .

The Complexity Trap

In the early stages of industry innovation, companies typically build new and better products through heavy investment in both product and process complexity. The product is hard to make, hard to use and expensive to produce. In the search for expansion, product variety, product proliferation, and customization are all vigorously pursued, greatly adding to the complexity of the firm's offering and operations. This is a natural path.

How do many ventures start? An entrepreneur innovates, turning an idea into a product that may be sold to other businesses. A viable solution is found and an initial customer is signed up. Whatever the customer wants — whatever adaptations and customization they demand — the new firm eagerly supplies. Keeping this precious customer happy therefore leads to increasing complexity. Soon, a second customer comes along, but they want different adaptations from the first one. More complexity. Then, in the quest to fill all possible niches — in the rational wish to exclude rivals and increase revenue — new products are created. New features and new technology are added in a hurry in order to provide a product for each segment. For instance, there may be a *luxury* version, an *eco* version, a *sports* version, a *baby* version, and so on. Adding features and technology seems entirely logical, and it helps to identify the venture with every aspect of the new market.

The complexity increasing is apparent in design, in

manufacturing, in selling, and in delivering an ever-widening range of products and services. When the firm has the ambition to expand, or when sales slow, the default mode is to increase complexity — more solutions, more varied products and customers, more customization, more markets and more diverse activity. There is constant pressure to come up with new ideas and managers are always excited by the "new new thing."

People who design complex products don't do it just for the hell of it. They are driven by a vision of how the products could be much more useful and attractive. The danger is that they get locked into the assumption that it is okay for the product or business system to become increasingly complex — heavier, more expensive, more convoluted, and harder for the uninitiated to use — as long as performance continues to improve.

At the start of its life cycle, the only way to improve a product is to add more resources and energy. After a while, though, this ceases to be true. It becomes possible to simplify — to make lighter, smaller products that have fewer features, are easier to use, cheaper to buy and operate, and less costly to produce and deliver. Yet managers who are used to progressing only by adding complexity often see simpler products not as a step forwards but as a step backwards.

There's another twist, too. Intelligent managers often instinctively prefer complexity to simplicity. For instance, engineers frequently relish the challenge of making a product that is more intricate than its predecessor. Moving upmarket appeals not only because margins are higher but because there is more opportunity to deploy expertise. So it takes a very resolute leader to convince managers that products should be simpler, not more elaborate. Simplifiers generally emerge from outside the mainstream — new entrepreneurs rather than corporate bigwigs. Short of cash, and often naturally inclined to parsimony, innovators such as Henry Ford, Sam Walton (the founder of Walmart), Ingvar Kamprad, Herb Kelleher, and Stelios Haji-Ioannou (the founder of EasyJet) are the natural exponents of simplicity, economy and the lowest-cost solution. Even when he was a billionaire, Walton drove himself everywhere in a car with over 100,000 miles on the odometer. The multi-billionaire Kamprad travels by bus or budget airline. Not many senior corporate leaders do likewise.

The Skills Trap

Theodore Levitt wrote one of the *Harvard Business Review*'s most famous articles — "Marketing Myopia" — back in 1960.[4] In this piece he argued that firms should meet customer needs rather than sell particular products. Thus, instead of thinking of itself specifically as a railroad, Penn Central should have acknowledged that it was in the transportation business. So, when air travel started to grow, it should have entered that market.

Business strategists have generally ridiculed this view. What did Penn Central know about running an airline? Products are where companies possess distinctive expertise and a reason to exist. So the final reason why managers are reluctant to simplify may appear to be a very good one — they don't have the skills or the culture required to enter a new market. Would it have made sense for America's leading chain of full-service restaurants to start McDonald's in 1948? Probably not. The skills that make a firm good at supplying a complex product or service often *disqualify* them for entering a far simpler market.

But consider three vignettes that point the other way.

In the 1980s, Hewlett-Packard quickly became the leading PC printer-maker, based on its expertise in sophisticated laser-jet printers. But when the simpler, slower, lower-resolution but much cheaper ink-jet printers started to dominate the market, HP set up an autonomous unit in Vancouver, Washington, which was allowed to compete with its own laser-jet business, based in Boise, Idaho. Thereafter, the classic pattern played out. The Boise operation went upmarket, producing ever more complex printers — larger, faster, and higher resolution. Of course, these were expensive, but they enjoyed fat margins. HP's Vancouver operation, meanwhile, steadily increased the speed of its ink-jet printers while keeping prices and costs low, which enabled it to compete with Canon and other new entrants. As ink-jet printers started to satisfy the demands of the mainstream, and laser-jet printers became a small segment at the very top of the market, HP was able to maintain its market leadership.[5]

The disk-drive industry boasts a rare example of a leader in an old product succeeding with a new, simpler one in the form of the Quantum Corporation and its spin-off, the Plus Development Corporation (PDC). Quantum was the leading manufacturer of 8-inch disk drives, but was stranded by the emergence of the simpler, cheaper 5.25-inch drive. The corporation introduced its own 5.25-inch product four years too late. However, in 1984, some Quantum employees decided to leave the firm, found PDC, and start making a 3.5-inch disk drive. Quantum offered to fund the new venture, securing 80 percent ownership. PDC designed the new drives but outsourced production to a division of Matsushita in Japan. Three years later, Quantum's sales of 8- and 5.25-inch drives had all but vanished, but it wisely bought the remaining fifth of PDC that it didn't already own, put the PDC executives in charge of the whole business, effectively shut down the old operation, but kept the Quantum brand.[6] The new Quantum went on to become the world's largest disk-drive supplier before selling out in 2001 and entering a third incarnation, this time as a leader in tape-storage products.

A final example. For decades, the Allen Bradley Company (AB) of Milwaukee was the leader in its field — it made rugged, heavy-duty, sophisticated, electromechanical switches to control large electric motors.[7] But these traditional controls were eventually threatened by smaller, simpler, cheaper, more flexible electronic motor controls. The first company to make these was Modicon, which started production in 1968. But the new technology was not seen as sufficiently robust or high performance for the users of electromechanical controls: machine-tool and crane manufacturers, and heating, ventilation and air-conditioning contractors. So Modicon sold its products to new customers, such as car-makers, who were starting to use motor controls in the process of factory automation.

If it had followed the well-worn script, AB would have continued to scorn the new technology until it was too late. Instead, though, it bought a quarter of Modicon's shares when the latter firm was just one year old. AB then bought the whole of another young electronic controls company and merged the two ventures. The new firm was kept separate from AB's traditional business and, indeed, competed with it. As electronic controls increasingly usurped electromechanical switches in U.S. factories, AB's four main rivals — including General Electric and Westinghouse — started to make their own electronic devices, but within their existing electrome-chanical operations. None of these four competitors proved successful in electronics, so AB maintained its dominance through its acquisition of the two startups.

The moral of these three stories is that the requirement for different skills is not necessarily a barrier to effective simplifying, provided the new skills are developed and kept *outside* the original operation, even after acquisition. As we saw earlier, one of the leading UK betting compa-nies would have been well advised to buy Betfair and its new electronic exchange technology at the start of this century, when it was a fledgling but fast-expanding com-pany. Perhaps companies such as Google — which rarely hesitates to buy businesses that are adjacent to its own — are right to do so, both to facilitate growth and to protect themselves from potential rivals.

Key Points

It is not that leading firms *cannot* simplify. Rather, there are deep managerial tendencies that make firms both *reluctant* and *slow* to do so:

1. The *Overhead Trap* — Companies have expectations about gross margins and are unwilling to develop prod-ucts that deviate either up or down from their existing overhead and margin levels.

2. The *Cannibalization Trap* — The leading firm does not want to eat its own lunch, which allows challengers to do it for them.

3. The *Customer Trap* — The firm rejects the new product because its best customers do.

4. The *Complexity Trap* — Managers naturally love complexity, or become accustomed to it, believing it is the only route to progress.

5. The *Skills Trap* — The firm may not have the right skills for simpler products, but it also fails to appreciate that these can be acquired, often quite cheaply.

There are, then, deep-rooted reasons why number-one firms usually do not simplify. But is managerial failure inevitable? Definitely not. There are many exceptions to the typical pattern. If the leaders of number-one firms understand what might happen, they can correct for the managerial bias towards complexity. In the next chapter, we look at what incumbents can do to simplify and stay ahead.

14

How Market Leaders Can Simplify Without Tears

The opportunity to secure ourselves against defeat lies in our own hands.

Sun Tzu

A simplifying firm emerges. Can the market leader stay on top? Of course it can, provided it has the right attitude and structure.

This is how a market leader can stay on top:

1. Determine whether your new rival is price- or proposition-simplifying.
2. Decide whether to respond by price- or proposition-simplifying yourself.
3. Commit to neutralizing the threat by simplifying more radically than they are.

4. **Adopt the structure that will maximize your chances of success. This means choosing *one* of the following five options:**

- *Develop and manufacture* the new, simple product alongside and within your existing organization. This nearly always fails! For example, DEC made its ill-fated PCs within the same organization as its core product — minicomputers.

- Abandon your existing, more complex product and *switch* entirely to developing the new simple product. This can work. For example, as we will see below, Kmart ditched its supermarket operation in the 1960s to focus exclusively on discount stores. Another example is McDonald's, which gave up its successful barbecue restaurant business and bet the farm on hamburgers.

- *Set up* a parallel, completely autonomous unit to supply the new, simple product. This can work, too, provided the new unit is allowed to be genuinely autonomous. Examples include HP's new ink-jet printer operation.

- *Sponsor* a spin-off to make the new, simple product. For example, Quantum's funding of the Plus Development Corporation.

- *Acquire* one or more of the new, simplifying firms. This is usually the strategy with the best chance of success. An example is the Allen Bradley Company, which acquired two startups in the electronic motor controls sector.

Countering Price-Simplifying

Intel

Intel Corporation invented the Dynamic Random Access Memory (DRAM) chip in 1969 and did very well with it for several years. By 1978, however, Japanese semiconductor makers were able to undercut the U.S. firm. A few years later, these low-cost rivals had put Intel in a very precarious position.

Intel saved itself by commissioning the development of the microprocessor, with the research, rather ironically, performed by a Japanese calculator-maker. Professor Clayton Christensen describes the microprocessor as follows:

"Mainstream as they seem today, microprocessors were disruptive technology when they first emerged. They were capable only of limited functionality … But they were small and simple, and they enabled affordable logic and computation in applications where this had not been feasible."[1]

In the 1960s, computers were powered by several integrated circuits, which used more electrical power, and generated more heat, than microprocessors. The latter were also smaller, higher performance, easier to incorporate into devices, and therefore easier for the machines' users. The Intel 4004, introduced in 1971, was the first commercial microprocessor, but it was some time before the corporation was able to make a viable product that could be used in numerous devices. (It eventually benefited from "Moore's

Law," which states that the number of components on a chip doubles every two years.) The big breakthrough came in 1981 when IBM decided to use the Intel 8088 microprocessor in its personal computer.[2] Shortly thereafter, Intel also supplied the "clones" — lower-cost PC-makers, such as Compaq — which soon overtook IBM. This strategy was spectacularly successful: Intel's market capitalization leapt from $4 billion to $197 billion between 1979 and 1987.

But the opportunities for breakthrough products are rare. If proposition-simplifying is impossible, the best response to a price-simplifier is to out-simplify that simplifier. I (Richard) had personal experience of this in the early 1990s.

Filofax

Filofax — the maker of iconic personal organizers before the days of digital organizers — had a great run from the 1960s to 1987, but then its sales and profits started to falter. The success of the company — and its high prices and profits — had invited lower-cost competition. In the UK, the main rival was Microfile, a price-simplifier offering an almost identical product for less than half the price.

As Filofax started to run out of cash, I organized a rescue bid and gained control of the company. The hypothesis was simple — since Microfile had price-simplified, Filofax should too. Microfile still had lower worldwide sales than Filofax, so we followed its cost-cutting measures: we replaced the leather folders with plastic and sourced cheaper paper from Scandinavia, while contracting out manufacturing and logistics. Filofax, we reckoned, should be able to get its costs below those of Microfile. We rationalized the product range down from several hundred to just four, and put most of our efforts into our new lead product — a "standard fill" of diary/calendar, Tube/subway maps, address book and notes. We also improved the design so the product was not only inexpensive but a joy to use.

Within three years, Filofax had quadrupled its volume and regained its market dominance. We sold the company for seven times what we had paid.

There was no significant change in either the product or the technology; and, as a single-product company, Filofax was relatively easy to turn around. But where the business model shifts fundamentally, it's a different story.

Woolco Versus Kmart

In the 1950s, F. W. Woolworth was the worldwide leader in general stores. It faced only one serious rival — S. S. Kresge — but the latter was stuck firmly in second place. Towards the end of the decade, however, a new retail format — discount stores — started to appear. These stores were the precursors, in concept if not in technology, of online retailers. They were price-simplifiers — with much lower prices and margins — but compensated by having far higher stock turns because the lower prices attracted customers.

F. W. Woolworth and S. S. Kresge opened their first discount stores in 1962, calling them Woolco and Kmart, respectively.[3] Kresge put all its money on the Kmart horse, closing its general stores. Woolworth decided to ride the two horses simultaneously within the organization. Initially, Woolco had its own discount store headquarters, but to save money it was later folded into the Woolworth general store regional structure. Under pressure from Woolworth's management, Woolco gradually raised its margins from 20 percent (similar to Kmart's) to 33 percent, much closer to the rest of Woolworth's.

Kmart's full commitment to the new business, and Woolworth's equivocal commitment, had a predictable result. By 1971, the former had revenues of $3.5 billion and a highly profitable business. By contrast, Woolco had sales below a billion and it was making no money. In 1982, it quit discount retailing altogether.

Sponsored Spin-Offs

So does setting up a separate division or operating site work? It certainly didn't for IBM or Woolworth, partly because, in both cases, when the going got tough, the parent company curbed the new division's autonomy. Yet, as we saw earlier, it did work for Hewlett-Packard, which did not restrict the new ink-jet division's autonomy. We also saw that the Plus Development Corporation was almost alone in making the transition to the simpler generation of disk drives. And, because its parent company Quantum sponsored the spin-off, retaining 80 percent of the equity, it was able to survive when its competitors in the 8-inch disk-drive market perished.

Sponsored spin-offs — where a firm retains a large stake in a new business — are rare, however. This is surprising, given that spin-offs have all the advantages of setting up an autonomous division, and several more besides:

- The individuals who propose and lead a spin-off are likely to be more entrepreneurial than the leaders of an autonomous unit, and they have greater motivation to make the new business valuable.
- After the initial set-up, the spin-off can raise money independently of the sponsoring corporation. This is perhaps the most important advantage. Though "autonomy" sounds great, the truth is that whoever controls the purse strings controls the operation. Financial independence is necessary for managerial independence.
- The sense of being masters of their own destiny is typically stronger for workers in a spin-off than for those in an autonomous unit within a big company. The absence of a corporate safety net tends to make spin-off executives more commercially focused and cash-conscious.
- A separate legal and ownership structure makes it all but impossible for the sponsoring corporation to lose its nerve and reincorporate the new unit.
- If the spin-off is kept totally separate, it can develop its own culture and rules of thumb that are better suited to simpler products and new customers. The spin-off is also more likely to develop an obsession with cost reduction as it will be unconstrained by any fear of cannibalization.
- Finally, the spin-off can offer a good home to an extremely talented but disruptive employee. For example, what if Steve Jobs and the Apple employees who founded NeXT had been "spun off" from Apple in 1985, with Apple retaining a significant stake in the new venture? (This is not a preposterous idea. Initially,

the Apple board proposed taking a 10 percent stake in Jobs' new business. He was in favor, but his fellow executives vetoed the idea.[4]) This would have made Jobs' exit from Apple a great deal smoother, and would have facilitated a much easier return to Apple when that was desperately needed a decade later.

Acquisition

A market leader facing a new simplifying firm may choose to buy the fledgling company rather than compete with it. This is particularly attractive when the technology or business model in the simplifying company is radically new, as it was with Betfair and the Allen Bradley Company. Buying the simplifier eliminates competition, gives the buyer a head start in the new business model, and serves as cheap insurance.

But a word of caution: acquisition may not work if the leader emasculates the acquired firm by interference. Keeping the latter separate and fully autonomous is essential for success. For example, Flickr was the undisputed leader in online photo-sharing when it was bought by Yahoo! in 2005, but then Yahoo! imposed a new set of objectives and tried to integrate Flickr into its corporate development processes. As a result, innovation was neglected, Facebook and Instagram filled the breach, and Flickr is now a shadow of its former self.[5]

Countering Proposition-Simplifying

As we have seen above, a market leader has several options when it comes to countering a price-simplifier. It is much harder to counter a proposition-simplifier.

With price-simplifying, the new approach should be evident almost as soon as it hits the market. If the leader chooses to play the new game, or at least hedge its bets, it will have the money and market presence to do so. Hence, in theory at least, it should be able to move faster than the start up, which will usually be short of both cash and experienced managers.

By contrast, you cannot counter a proposition-simplifying product if you are unaware of it. The new product may be in development and lurking in the shadows for several years before it is revealed in all its glory. Once that happens, it may take the leader several years to replicate the product, and by then the newcomer may have seized first-mover advantage, locked in customers, established distribution and scale advantages, and cemented its brand identity within the new market category.

Consequently, leading firms have rarely managed to fend off innovators with a simpler product that is truly a joy to use.

In 1995, AltaVista proposition-simplified, introducing a search engine that was faster and more comprehensive than any other. As a result, it quickly became number one in online search engines, and one of the early internet's most visited sites. But when Google came along with an engine that was even quicker, simpler, more accurate and easier to use, AltaVista fell away very quickly. Neither Compaq nor Yahoo! — each of which acquired the firm — could save it.

Similarly, as soon as the Sony Walkman appeared, it seized market leadership in the stereo player market, seeing off first Stereobelt — an invention of the German–Brazilian entrepreneur Andreas Pavel — and then Toshiba, Aiwa, and Panasonic. The Walkman was the simplest product on the market and a joy to use.

The Austrian entrepreneur Dietrich Mateschitz created Red Bull in 1987. His product was a simplified version of an existing Thai drink which he marketed as an "energy drink" (this was Mateschitz's truly innovative idea). Then he put it in a beautiful, tall, thin, silver–blue can and rolled the drink out rapidly throughout the Western world. Since then, many lower-price versions have achieved some success, but none has toppled Red Bull. This has parallels with the Coke versus Pepsi battle, in which the latter price-simplified and seized part of the market, but never became top dog.

A similar pattern occurred with smartphones. Nokia, the dominant maker of mobile phones for over a decade, was swept aside by Apple. Then, with its cheaper products, Samsung challenged Apple, especially in Europe. Yet, from its launch in 2007 to at least 2012, the iPhone was both the U.S. and the global market leader, despite its phones costing far more than any of their rivals.

Counter Price- *and* Proposition-Simplifying

A market leader is rarely assailed simultaneously by *both* price- and proposition- simplifiers. But, as we have seen, IBM was in the mid-1980s. When the Apple Macintosh appeared, IBM did not even try to make a machine that was more intuitive and easy to use. Around the same time, it also lost out to price-simplifiers — HP, Compaq, and Dell.

IBM could have done something to counter these threats: it could have bought Apple in 1982 and put all of its energy into proposition-simplifying. Instead, it tried to straddle two utterly incompatible strategies and failed miserably at both.

Is the Penny Dropping About Acquiring Proposition-Simplifiers?

Right now, several firms in Silicon Valley seem particularly keen to buy up smaller competitors who might become threats as proposition-simplifiers.

Waze was founded in 2008 with the aim of pioneering a new generation of GPS software that would collect information about traffic jams from users and provide real-time updates. Once developed, this free, proposition-simplified service was a true joy to use — far simpler and more practical than traditional GPS. Google bought Waze in 2013 for $996 million.

The video-sharing website YouTube launched in 2005 and Google bought it the very next year. Network effects have since given YouTube a huge lead in its market, and it will probably never be replicated because it hosts the content. When Google acquired the service, YouTube's growth was exponential because its videos were instantly approved, whereas Google's sat in limbo for three days, awaiting approval. This delay killed vitality and spontaneity. YouTube, by contrast, was a joy-to-use proposition-simplifier. It is also now the world's second-biggest search engine (after Google itself).

By buying these and other businesses that were adjacent to its core search engine operation, Google has increased its dominance in searching and has built a buffer against competition in that market.

Finally, launched in 2009, WhatsApp is a cross-platform texting subscription service. By April 2014, it had 500 million active users and handled more than 10 billion text messages every day, with 700 million photos and 100 million videos shared daily. Six months later, Facebook bought its rival for a stunning $19 billion — another example of acquiring a dominant proposition-simplifier.

Key Points

1. To repulse a simplifier, the leading firm should commit to providing the purest possible form of either price- or proposition-simplifying. Then it must adopt the structure that maximizes its chances of doing that.
2. Acquisition is often the best and simplest way to do this, provided you can resist the temptation to interfere afterwards.
3. It is easier to counter price-simplifying than proposition-simplifying. In the latter case, early acquisition of the simplifier is sometimes the *only* option if the market leader is to avoid catastrophe.

To identify the best option for your company if you are facing a simplifying rival, visit www.SIMPLIFYforCEOs. com.

We now turn to the final part of the book, in which we ask if simplifying really makes a big difference to financial returns.

PART FOUR

The Rewards of Simplifying

In this final part, we look at the returns from both price- and proposition-simplifying. Then we conduct a little "archaeological dig" to probe why returns may be high or low, before exploring the limitations, power and glory of simplifying.

15

Does Price-Simplifying Pay?

We will make electricity so cheap that only the rich will burn candles.

Thomas Edison

How good are the returns from price-simplifying? What do our case studies indicate about the conditions for success and how far it can go?

To shed some light on the financial rewards of simplifying, we asked OC&C Strategy Consultants to examine the twelve case studies — six price-simplifiers and six proposition-simplifiers — that they consider the most significant simplifiers since 1900. In this chapter we look at the results for the price-simplifiers; in the next we look at those for the proposition-simplifiers. OC&C's findings are not guarantees that similar patterns will occur in the future, but the twelve case studies are at least highly suggestive.

The six price-simplifiers have all appeared in earlier chapters, but here we focus on the impact of price-simplifying on their respective fortunes and the size of their markets.

Ford

You may recall from Chapter 1 that Henry Ford started simplifying in 1906. A period of huge expansion followed, as Ford's focus on a single car led to the Model T and to investment in the world's largest factory to produce it on a massive scale. But the big breakthrough came in 1913, when the moving assembly line replaced batch production. Through basic but excellent design, and by reducing his prices every year, Ford had no problem selling all his output, even though the latter increased by between 47 and 117 percent every year until 1917, when some of the company's manufacturing was diverted into war work.

This phase of rapid market expansion through rolling out ever-cheaper Model Ts began to lose momentum in 1920. Although Ford set a new record that year by selling 1.25 million cars, the rate of growth began to decline thereafter as the newly merged General Motors shifted the basis of competition from price to model innovation by offering greater style, variety, and improved features to more affluent customers. OC&C therefore decided to study only the years 1906–20 in order to measure the initial, profound effect of Ford's price-simplifying. Ford's prices fell by 76 percent between 1906 and 1920, which was all the more impressive considering that consumer prices more than doubled in the same period (the Consumer Price Index increased by 130 percent). Yet the company's revenue rose from under

$2.4 million in 1906 to \$359 million in 1920 — a 150-fold increase. The number of cars the firm sold each year increased even more impressively — by 782 times — and its market share (by units) rocketed from 8 percent in 1906 to between 75 and 80 percent in 1920 (dollar market share was slightly lower at between 65 and 70 percent).

Ford's unit market volume increased by over 500 times, and its market value rose by 150 times, compared with just a ninefold increase for the companies that later merged into General Motors, Ford's most serious competitor(s) both from 1906 to 1920 and for most of the rest of the twentieth century. The figure for "value outperformance" — the number of times Ford's value increased relative to the number of times its closet rival's value increased — is therefore 17 (150 ÷ 9). In absolute terms, the company's surge in value compounded at 43 percent annually between 1906 and 1920.

All of these astonishing achievements are summarized in Figure 6.

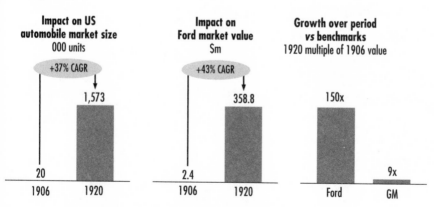

Figure 6: Ford's early growth

As is well known, the Ford Motor Company was very badly managed from the 1920s and for most of the rest of the century. It lost market leadership to GM in 1935, failed to continue price-simplifying, failed to make the adjustment to proposition-simplifying, failed to reinvent the low-cost car in the way that both the Volkswagen Beetle and the BMC Mini did, and — for more than a decade — failed to match the quality standards of Toyota and other Asian car-makers.

Therefore, it is intriguing that, taking the whole period from 1906 to the present day, Ford's market value increased by more than 24,451 times, at a compound annual growth rate of 10 percent. GM's value increased "only" 500 times, so Ford's value outperformance figure over the long term (albeit against a rival that eventually turned out to have feet of clay) is 49. This suggests that the brand equity created by Henry Ford by being the *first* price-simplifier — by "democratizing the automobile," as he put it — was so massive that it endured for more than a century and continued to generate above-average financial returns over that whole period (see Figure 7). As we will see later, this pattern — a firm gaining an extremely long-lasting advantage from early innovation — is evident in other industries, too.

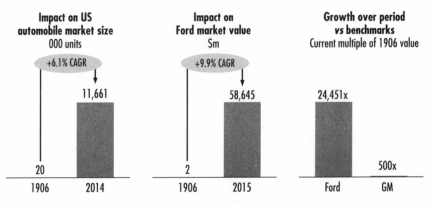

Figure 7: Ford's growth over a century

McDonald's

In 1948 the McDonald brothers converted their conventional barbecue restaurant into a production line not unlike Henry Ford's. They used their "speedee service" to provide high-quality hamburgers at half their competitors' price — fifteen cents instead of thirty. As we saw in Chapter 3, the McDonalds price-simplified by narrowing their menu to just nine items, by buying the ingredients for those few items in bulk, by persuading the customers to serve themselves, and by collapsing the time taken to cook and deliver the food so that they could serve far more customers without the need to move to larger premises or take on extra staff. It was a beautifully simple economic revolution.

The financial rewards soon followed. The profit in 1948, the first year of the "new" McDonald's, was approximately $50,000, and the value of the San Bernardino business at the end of that year was $237,000.[1] Thirteen years later, Ray Kroc's consortium bought the whole business — which now comprised thirteen restaurants — for $2.7 million, so McDonald's value grew 11.4 times between 1948 and 1961 — a compound annual growth rate of 20.6 percent (see Figure 8). Of course, this calculation does not include the increase in value between 1947 and 1948 due to the conversion to the new hamburger restaurant model. Since we know that this more than doubled the company's revenues, it seems reasonable to assume that the real uplift from the new system was at least double the 1948–61 calculation.

OC&C next analyzed McDonald's increase in market value between 1961 and 2014, due to Ray Kroc and his successors rolling out the simple McDonald's formula across

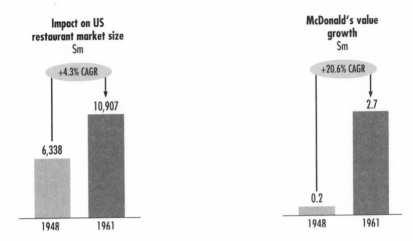

Figure 8: McDonald's early growth

the United States and then the world. The company's value in 2015 was $93 billion, a 34,627-fold increase since 1961, or a compound annual increase of 21 percent. There was no comparable restaurant chain during this period, so OC&C compared the McDonald's increase to the Standard & Poor's (S&P) 500 index over the same period, which increased by 28 times (Figure 9). Therefore, McDonald's registered a 1249-times value outperformance over the S&P index.

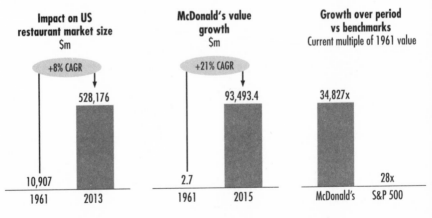

Figure 9: McDonald's growth to the present day

This impressive performance was based on McDonald's amazing revenue growth (which increased by 10,554 times between 1961 and 2015), on an expansion of margins, and on the multiple of market value to profits growing. Roughly speaking, the revenue increase was multiplied by three to arrive at the market value increase.

But McDonald's would not be worth anything like its current value without that exponential increase in revenue over the last fifty-four years. What does this imply about market growth? OC&C found that the U.S. restaurant market increased in value from $10.9 billion in 1961 to $526.2 billion in 2013, an increase of more than 42 times, and an annual compound increase of 8 percent. But, of course, this massively understates the real growth in the McDonald's, Burger King and Wendy's type of operation — "fast-hamburger" restaurants — in the United States and around the world. If we assume that McDonald's had roughly 95 percent of this fast-hamburger market in 1961, and that today it has roughly 50 percent of it globally, then the increase in market size becomes more than 20,000 times — a compound annual increase of 20 percent sustained over more than half a century.[2] That is quite an increase to result from a simplified retail format and a 50 percent price cut!

Southwest Airlines

In Chapter 10 we traced the story of Herb Kelleher's creation, Southwest Airlines. In 1971 the new airline charged only twenty dollars for a trip between Dallas and San Antonio or Houston, a cut of 65 percent compared with previous average fares. Southwest's IPO in 1971 valued the company at just $6.5 million. Eight years later, Southwest was making a healthy operating profit of $29 million on a turnover of $136 million, and the company was valued at $61.9 million. This 9.5-fold increase in Southwest's value compared to a 40 percent *decline* in value for American Airlines and a near standstill in the S&P 500, which increased by a mere 10 percent over the same period. Total industry revenues nearly tripled in these eight years, nearly all the full-service airlines were unable to increase their profits (see Figure 10).

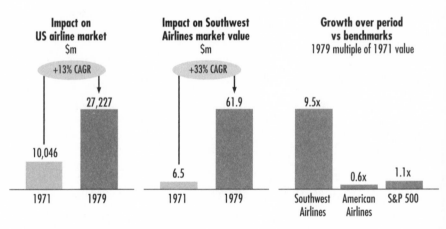

Figure 10: Southwest Airlines' growth in the 1970s

In 1979, the U.S. airline market was deregulated and Southwest expanded hugely as it was "THE low-cost airline." By 2011, it had become the number-one U.S. airline by passengers carried, and three years later its revenues were 137 times higher than they had been in 1979 (at $18.6 billion). Its market value increased even more over the same period — by 468 times — to $29 billion. This compares with increases in American Airlines' value (from a very low base in 1979) of 74 times and in the benchmark S&P 500 index of only 19 times (see Figure 11). Once again, a price-simplifier demonstrated huge value growth and significant outperformance over the long term by rolling out a formula it had established in its first few years.

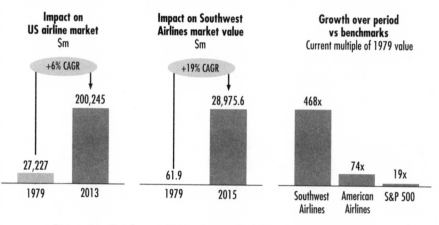

Figure 11: Southwest Airlines' growth, 1979 to the present day

IKEA

As we saw in Chapter 2, Ingvar Kamprad simplified the furniture industry through a proprietary system which lowered cost at every point, not least through IKEA's innovation of flat-pack furniture assembled at home by the customer, leading to huge savings in transport costs (which can comprise up to half of total product costs in the traditional furniture industry). Kamprad insisted on engineering products down to prices that were 50–80 percent lower than before.

Between its founding in 1958 and 1974, IKEA's expansion in Scandinavia led to a 56-times increase in both revenue and market value, an increase of 29 percent each year — although calculating the true value of IKEA, a private company which is as parsimonious with its financial data as it is with its product costings, is notoriously difficult. We know, however, that IKEA's revenue in 2014 was €29.3 billion, a mammoth 173 times higher than in 1974, when the company first started to conquer the world's furniture markets. The group's declared operating income in 2014 was €3.793 billion, though this excludes the "franchise fee" of 3 percent of revenue levied by Inter IKEA Systems. If this amount — €879 million — is added to the operating profit, and a conservative multiple of ten is then applied, we arrive at a total "economic value" of IKEA of some €46.7 billion.[3] This would imply a value that is also 173 times higher than in 1974, a compound annual increase of 14.1 percent (Figure 12).

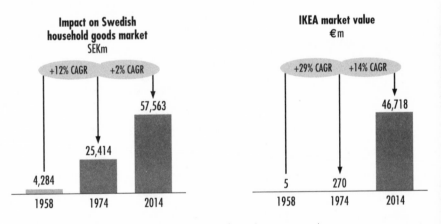

Figure 12: IKEA's growth to the present day

Yet again, price-simplifying seems to have produced excellent growth in market value over several decades. Intuitively, we may understand this as being due to the interaction of two price-simplifying characteristics. The first of these is competitive security and therefore solid margins, because no rival can attain the same scale and hence the same low-cost position. Despite its very low prices, IKEA still has operating margins above 15 percent — more than twice as high as those of its main rivals.

The second big advantage of price-simplifying is that it lends itself to growth through internationalization, which dramatically increases revenues while also enhancing scale and margin benefits. Even though its growth is now slowing, over the last quarter-century or so IKEA's annual revenue growth has been 14 percent, whereas the rest of the industry has grown by a mere 2 percent.

Charles Schwab

In 1975 the U.S. Securities and Exchange Commission removed limits on brokerage commissions, and Charles Schwab slashed its brokerage rates by 80 percent. Later, the firm reduced them to less than a tenth of what they had been originally. As we saw in Chapter 11, the firm automated its system, and in 1982 it became the first to offer 24/7 direct access to the stock market.

Ever since, Schwab has remained the market leader in discount brokerage and the firm has benefited hugely from the market explosion that it catalyzed. The market grew from $7.4 billion in 1975 to $272 billion in 2014, an increase of 37 times, equating to 10 percent a year compounded. Meanwhile, the value of Charles Schwab grew even more impressively — from just $100,000 to $43.5 billion by 2015 — a 435,471-fold increase, equating to an average compound annual increase of 38 percent. The firm's closest competitor, though neither a discount broker nor a price-simplifier, is Merrill Lynch, which increased by just 48 times over the *whole period*. Charles Schwab therefore wins the "outperformance in value creation" competition between our six price-simplifiers, as it performed 9165 times better than its nearest rival. In the outperformance stakes, it truly is in a class of its own. (Remember that Ford outperformed its nearest rival — GM — by "only" 49 times over the last century.)

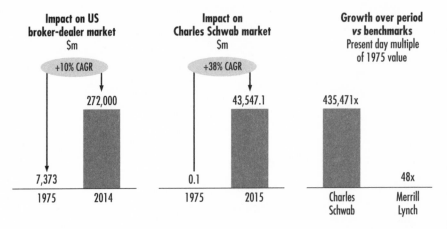

Figure 13: Charles Schwab's growth

The Charles Schwab story reinforces the theme that price-simplifier success can last for a very long time. It is telling that the firm's profits declined only once, in 2004, after the eponymous founder of the firm — "Chuck" Schwab — stepped down as CEO and his long-time deputy David Pottruck took over for a year. Pottruck went against the firm's heritage by increasing prices, and he was punished by a 26 percent fall in trading revenue. The founder took up the reins again, cancelled the commission increases, and took the firm to greater heights by driving fees even lower.

Honda

As we saw in Chapter 8, Honda's initial mistake was to disregard its marvelous little bike — the 50cc Supercub — when it first attempted to break into the U.S. motorcycle market. The firm soon corrected this error on the advice of Kihachiro Kawashima,[4] but it could have avoided months of turmoil (and almost zero sales) if it had followed one basic price-simplifying rule from the outset:

- If you have a well-designed, low-cost product that can be sold for half the price of a comparable product, go for it, even if that rival product is technically superior.

The comparable products in this case were U.S. (and later UK) low-power motorcycles. Honda's bikes were approximately 70–80 percent lower in price than these rival products. Clearly not all buyers of the more expensive domestic products considered a Japanese 50cc bike acceptable, but enough of them did for Honda to establish a viable foothold in the U.S. market.

The Supercub had lower performance than its rivals, but it also offered great value for money. BCG's 1975 report into the British motorcycle industry showed that Honda's labor costs per bike were approximately one-tenth of those in the UK for bikes of similar performance, even though Honda paid its workers 45 percent more! The Japanese company was able to do this partly through higher scale but mainly through superior design and lower production costs. As the report said,

"It is often said that Honda created the market in the United State and elsewhere — for what we have called secondary uses of motorcycles — through their extensive advertising and promotion activities; and it is true that Honda presented the attractions of motorcycling as a 'fun' activity in a new way ... However, the success of this campaign depended in the last resort on the fact that the lightweight machines that were then the company's primary product *were* fun and easy to use, did not give the mechanical problems that had traditionally been associated with motorcycles, and were cheap to purchase."[5]

We saw in Chapter 8 that Honda's entry into the U.S. market was the catalyst for a tenfold increase in market size between 1959 and 1975. In that period the company also started to make more powerful bikes, helped by its modular bike-component design. This forced established British bike-makers — such as Norton Villiers Triumph — into bankruptcy. The Japanese then forced Harley-Davidson, the U.S. market leader, into progressive "segment retreat," with the U.S. firm obliged to focus on ever-larger bikes, the only ones where Honda did not have the edge.

OC&C's analysis shows that Honda's market value increased by 377 times between 1959 and 2015, compared with a "mere" 33-fold increase for its main competitor, Harley-Davidson — an outperformance of 11 times (see Figure 14).

Honda took a similar price-simplifying approach in cars and other areas, exploiting its simple engine technology to the maximum extent.

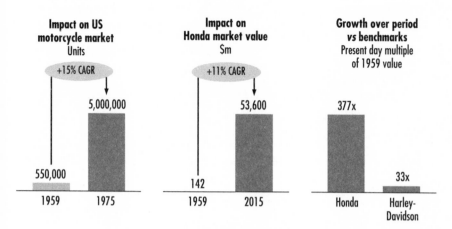

Figure 14: Honda's growth

Just six case studies cannot be statistically significant, but the parallels between them are certainly interesting.

- In every case, halving prices multiplied the market size; and if defined narrowly (as with fast hamburgers), this could more than double every two years for more than half a century, rising tens of thousands of times.
- In every case, the revenues of the price-simplifier rose by several thousand times (and in one case by 280,000 times).
- In every case, the value of the company rose sharply, with increases measured in the tens, hundreds, thousands, tens of thousands, or (again in one case) hundreds of thousands.
- In every case, the compound annual growth rate of value increased impressively, ranging from 10 percent a year over more than a century to 40 percent a year over four decades.

- In every case, outperformance relative to a comparable non-simplifying company or the stock market was also striking, varying from 11 times to over 9000 times.
- In every case, the value increase continued over several decades, even when the company stopped innovating or cutting prices.

Let us now see whether the story is any different for the six proposition-simplifying companies which OC&C selected for analysis.

Does Proposition-Simplifying Pay?

Once the [iPod] project was launched, Jobs immersed himself in it daily. His main demand was "Simplify!" He would go over each screen of the user interface and apply a rigid test: he should be able to get there in three clicks. And the click should be intuitive. If he couldn't figure out how to navigate to something, or if it took more than three clicks, he would be brutal.[1]

Walter Isaacson

What do the six proposition-simplifying case studies tell us? Does proposition-simplifying pay as impressively as price-simplifying?

Amazon

We start with a small dilemma. Is Amazon an example of price-simplifying, proposition-simplifying, or both?

We have decided to classify the company as a proposition-simplifier because it made book shopping (and then shopping in general) so much easier. There are four elements to this:

- First, Amazon pioneered online book sales (and later sales in other categories), offering extraordinary range and the convenience of buying almost anything immediately, without the need to visit a store.
- Second, Amazon's patented "1-click" system made it even easier to buy.
- Third, Amazon's reviews and suggestions provide a wealth of information to inform the purchase decision (and to stimulate users to buy more). Once again, the company was the principal pioneer of this system and its process has been greatly imitated but rarely improved.
- Finally, the creation of the Amazon marketplace has allowed other sellers to play along, which has enhanced convenience and increased product range for the consumer.

So Amazon makes it a joy to shop, principally through greater ease of use, so it is clearly a proposition-simplifier.

But it also offers unbeatable prices. So is it also a price-simplifier?

OC&C calculated that Amazon offers an average 32.7 percent discount on list price of popular (physical) books, and an average 53 percent discount for Kindle books compared with list price of the cheapest physical book equivalent. This clearly does not meet our basic requirement that price-simplifiers must cut prices in half, although it is not a million miles away. But perhaps retailers should be viewed as a special case, because their cost of goods — what they must buy before they sell — is so much higher as a proportion of final sales price than that of most businesses. The true measure (for all businesses) should be the proportion of "value-added" that price-simplifiers remove in a price cut. The value-added for Amazon on books is not much more than what they pass on to the customer in price reduction. The proof is that Amazon.com currently operates on a net operating profit margin of just 1 percent of sales, whereas most retailers (including other online retailers) operate on margins of between 3 and 15 percent.

As we saw earlier, the bane of the proposition-simplifier's existence is that its rivals may imitate its joy-to-use innovations ... and Amazon is no exception. Everyone can now sell with one click, post online reviews and offer recommendations. Many sites can now boast an enormously wide variety of certain goods. Rivals have copied Amazon's Kindle — both the hardware and the software — numerous times. Unsurprisingly, then, although Amazon's massive customer base, enviable service levels, wide range within and between product categories and broad marketplace for third-party sellers still give it an edge, its proposition advantage is eroding. So it might eventually be viewed as more of a price- than a proposition-simplifier, or even as that rarest of beasts — *both* a price-simplifier and a proposition-simplifier. Nevertheless, since it started as a proposition-simplifier, we have included it in this chapter.

So, what effect has Amazon had on its market over the past two decades?

By value, the online book market has grown by an average of 21 percent each year since the launch of Amazon in 1995. Amazon still enjoys the dominant share of that market (with 63 percent of all *online* book sales and 40 percent of *total* book sales),[2] but its growth in other sectors has been even more impressive. Since the company's expansion into consumer electronics and other products — and into offering its proposition-simplifying online expertise to other merchants, including Marks & Spencer and Lacoste — its revenues have soared, multiplying 176,000 times between 1997 and 2014, meaning they have more than doubled each year (a compound annual growth rate of 104 percent). Moreover, Amazon's market value multiplied over 55,000 times between 1995 and 2015 — a stunning annual growth rate of 73 percent. This compares with a 1.1-times growth for Barnes & Noble, the previous market leader in bookselling, and 3.4 times for the S&P 500 index over the same period (see Figure 15). Amazon's outperformance value (against the index) is therefore 16,448 (and, of course, it is even higher against its chief rival).

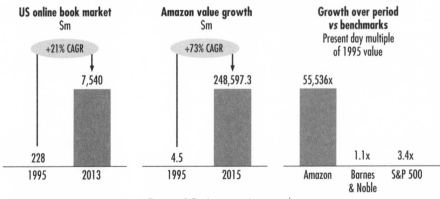

Figure 15: Amazon's growth

Can You Be Both a Price- and a Proposition-Simplifier?

In normal market conditions, where there is a level playing field for all competitors, the answer is a resounding "No!" For our purposes, we somewhat arbitrarily define "normal market conditions" as a time when there is a low rate of technological change, so all competitors have relatively equal access to the principal technologies of production and marketing, and newer technologies are well diffused. In addition, under normal market conditions, there are no strong non-market phenomena at work, such as stringent government regulation and the like.

We'll explain why this matters shortly, but first it is evident that there are some fundamental differences between price- and proposition-simplifying business models under normal market conditions. Let's examine price-simplifying first.

As we know, price-simplifying is defined by a single overriding objective — clear cost and price leadership. A unitary and relatively rigid business form then flows organically from this single purpose. There is no segmentation — the market is the largest-possible mass market. There are no material product attribute trade-offs against lowest price. There are no radically different ways of achieving the scale economics needed to deliver lowest price. For instance, UK/Irish budget airlines use exactly the same technologies as and bear an uncanny resemblance to U.S. budget airlines. Achieving the price imperative requires highest scale, and this informs every choice in the design of the business and production system. This quest for scale leads to integrated and inflexible linkages in the production system and supply chain in order to coordinate higher throughput. Capital equipment is introduced to automate production and eliminate labor, but this requires heavy investment. These assets have long productive lives and long payback periods, meaning the enterprise is even more tied to a rigid modus operandi over an extended period of time, again limiting flexibility.

Proposition-simplifying is very different because the company has to respond to several variables, not just price. Here the simplifier targets one of several possible large segments, or clusters of segments, and positions the product or service depending on the appropriate permutation of utility, ease of use, and aesthetic appeal for that target market. A different combination of attributes might be chosen by competitors attempting to encroach, outflank, or re-segment the position that the product simplifier has chosen. This leads to product contention and product evolution driven by competition. For example, the iPhone established the benchmark in smartphones; then Samsung emulated the basic concept but with a larger screen; then Apple responded with its own larger-screen version. So the iPhone ended up as a *family* of products in order to defend its territory from competitive differentiation.

This need to respond to competitive differentiation means that the simplifier has to maintain production flexibility and not optimize for price. Fortunately, it can afford to do so because a leading simplified proposition can sustain a premium price and high profit margins, which in turn allow for flexibility and responsiveness in the production system. In many cases production is outsourced to maintain maximum flexibility. There is not the same degree of business system simplification, rigidity, integration, design for scale capacity and cost optimization as with a price-simplifier. This would be inappropriate, too dangerous, too limiting on the product side; it would leave the proposition-simplifier too exposed to competition. Hence, the proposition-simplifier needs to focus its main effort on producing by far the simplest and most appealing offering in an evolving field, *not* on developing a business system with a sharp focus on reducing cost.

In a normal market the two strategies therefore lead to two very different, incompatible business conditions and requirements. But what if we were to abandon the assumption that technology is stable, with equal access for all?

Imagine you are the inventor of the wheel. You go down to the local patent office and secure the exclusive legal right to use and apply your invention for a long time. That puts you in a rather interesting position. Having unequal access to this extraordinary new technology allows you to produce all manner of products that are fundamentally *better* propositions than their predecessors — donkeys and horses, canal boats, litters, Sherpas and so on — but also much *cheaper.* Your groundbreaking invention has enabled you to be *both* a price- and a proposition-simplifier! Exclusive access to a dramatically better idea or technology is the condition that allows a firm to follow both strategies successfully.

But a word of warning for our wheel entrepreneur and his successors: *all technologies diffuse over time.* So, at some point in the future, you will need to choose just one strategy and abandon the other. If you do not, your competitors will eventually out-price- and out-proposition-simplify you, and you will be stuck between two incompatible paths.

Google

As mentioned earlier, Google's story is remarkable. The search engine the company launched in 1998 was so much easier and quicker to use than any of its rivals that it rapidly wiped the market leader, AltaVista, off the map. In an echo of other successful proposition-simplifiers, the art lay in concealing the complexity of the internal process (in this case, Google's algorithm) from users, and making the product seem incredibly simple.

Since then, Google has changed the world of advertising, and with it the whole media world. Between 1997 — the last year BG (Before Google) — and 2015, the global internet advertising market soared from $907 million to $171 billion — an astounding annual growth rate of 34 percent. But Google's value soared even faster — compounded annually at 135 percent — to reach nearly $200 billion by 2015 (see Figure 16).

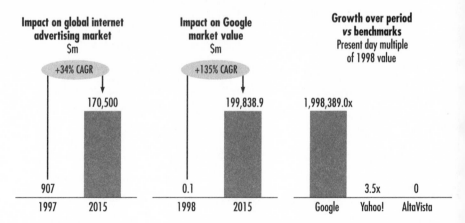

Figure 16: Google's growth

Google's value grew by almost *two million times* between 1998 and 2015 — by far the highest rate of any of our case studies. Over the same period, early rival AltaVista became defunct, the S&P 500 index grew by 1.7 times, and Yahoo! displayed a 3.5-fold increase. Google's value outperformance figure when measured against its closest rival (Yahoo!) was nearly 600,000. This reflects the fact that online network markets are very much winner-takes-all environments — the most popular site gains a dominant market share, whether for reasons of liquidity, because everyone wants to use the site everyone else is using, or because the site obviously offers the best proposition. Google's outperformance of its rivals also reflects the incredibly short time period — just sixteen years — during which it became so valuable. No other company in history (even adjusting for inflation) has become worth so much so quickly.

Apple (the iPod Years)

Apple was founded on 1 April 1976. As we saw earlier, it made its fortune with the first popular "modern" computer, the Macintosh, in 1984. Then the company lost its way after Steve Jobs was forced out the following year, and by 1997 it was almost bankrupt. However, Jobs' "Second Coming" towards the end of that year began a remarkable period of pruning and kick-started the firm's renaissance. Jobs focused on just two models of the Mac and returned Apple to profit by producing the easiest-to-use, most fun personal computer on the market. But the growth in that niche was limited, and breaking into the mass computer market was not an option (at the time the company had only a 4 percent unit market share in computers). Apple was a proposition-simplifier, not a price-simplifier.

So what could Jobs do? The strategy professor Richard Rumelt recounts meeting Apple's CEO in 1998 and telling him, in effect, that he was boxed into a corner. "He did not attack my argument," Rumelt remembers. "He didn't agree with it, either. He just smiled and said, 'I am going to wait for the next big thing.'"[3]

That next big thing, as we now know, was the iPod — another extraordinary example of proposition-simplifying. It began with iTunes, launched in January 2001. As the Apple team played around with hooking up existing MP3 players to their new platform, they found the machines — in the words of Jon Rubenstein — "horrible, absolutely horrible." Another iTunes team member, Phil Schiller, said, "These things really stink. They hold about sixteen songs, and you can't figure out how to use them."[4] So began the intensive process whereby, in less than a year, Jobs and the team devised a far simpler player. As his biographer recounts,

"The most Zen of all simplicities was Jobs' decree, which astonished his colleagues, that the iPod would not have an on–off switch ... Suddenly everything had fallen into place: a drive that would hold a thousand songs; an interface and scroll wheel that would let you navigate a thousand songs; a FireWire connection that could sync a thousand songs in under ten minutes; and a battery that would last through a thousand songs. 'We suddenly were looking at one another and saying, this is going to be so cool,' Jobs recalled. 'We knew how cool it was, because we knew how badly we each wanted one personally. And the concept became so beautifully simple: a thousand songs in your pocket.'"[5]

Lighter, more stylish and elegant, and much easier to use than any other music player, the iPod was an overnight sensation. The enthusiasm of Jobs and his team resulted in a product as great as it was simple. But did it make the firm any money?

Between 2001 and the next great Apple innovation in 2007 — the iPhone — the worldwide market for portable media players grew by 160 percent, an annual increase of 17.6 percent. Apple's product astonished the nerds with its price as much as its technical excellence — at $399 it was by far the most expensive portable music player on the market. The joke on the internet was that iPod meant "Idiots Price Our Devices."[6] As we have seen throughout this book, however, proposition-simplifiers who have a genuine breakthrough product can extract their pound of flesh: unlike price-simplifiers, they do not have to accept a trade-off between growth and margins.

In just six years, Apple's total revenues increased by 4.5 times, and the firm's market value exploded from $7.6 billion to $167 billion — a 22-fold increase, equal to a compound

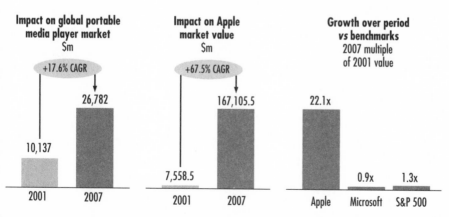

Figure 17: Apple's growth after the launch of the iPod

annual growth rate of 68 percent. By contrast, Microsoft's value *declined* slightly, and the S&P 500 index rose only marginally, by 1.3 times (see Figure 17).

ARM

Advanced RISC Machines, a joint venture between Acorn Computers, Apple, and VLSI Technology, was founded in 1990. Eight years later, it changed its name to ARM Holdings and was floated on both the London and NASDAQ stock exchanges. Based in "Silicon Fen" (Cambridge, England), ARM is a proposition-simplifier that designs products — specifically lighter, less power-intensive semiconductor chips — and then licenses them to manufacturers of mobile phones and tablets. It therefore has a symbiotic relationship with the markets for these products — especially the smartphone market — both accelerating their growth through its innovative designs and benefiting from that growth itself. In 1997 sales of chips containing ARM cores stood at nine million. By 2013, that figure had rocketed to ten billion — an annual increase of 55 percent. In 2010, chips designed by ARM accounted for 95 percent of all chips in smartphones.[7]

ARM's market value in 1998 was a shade over $1 billion. By 2015, it had increased 19 times — to $19.773 billion — an annual growth rate of 20 percent. This compares with increases of 1.1 times for Intel (which both designs and makes chips) and 1.7 times for the S&P 500 index over the same period (see Figure 18).

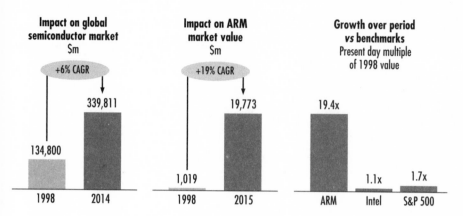

Figure 18: ARM's growth

Tetra Pak

Ruben Rausing founded the Swedish company Tetra Pak in 1951. His mantra was that "a package must save more than it costs" — the saving for dairies and other liquid-food manufacturers must be greater than the price Tetra Pak charged for the packaging. This was made possible by the invention of a new tetrahedron-shaped pack, initially for storing cream and milk, and also by the introduction of new machines that could use Tetra Pak's unique laminated material and do the packing on site at dairies and juice-makers. It took Rausing more than a decade to perfect these innovations, but then his business took off.

Tetra Pak's technological innovations make the factory filling and packing, transportation, and stacking on supermarket shelves so much easier for the company's customers — the dairies and juice producers. The packs costs more than conventional containers, yet customers save more money than they pay Tetra Pak. This is achieved because there is less need for refrigeration, spoilage is reduced, and transportation, storage and disposal costs are all cut. Tetra Pak says that the typical cost reduction for a dairy or juicer is around 12 percent of operating costs — a large sum, but not nearly enough to make the company a price-simplifier. Yet the advantages that accrue to the company's customers in terms of ease of use, greater speed in production, and logistics — as well as further advantages for its customers' customers (supermarkets) — fully justify calling Tetra Pak a proposition-simplifier.

The Institute of Food Technologists called the aseptic "Tetra Brik", introduced in 1963, the most important food-packaging innovation of the twentieth century.[8] And when Niels Bohr, one of the greatest physicists of all time, visited the company's factory and research-and-development facilities in Lund, he said that he had never seen "such an adequate practical application of a mathematical problem."[9]

By sticking to its packaging mission and continually improving the products it offers to its customers, Tetra Pak has become the largest and most profitable food-packaging

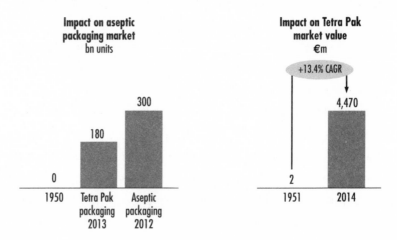

Figure 19: Tetra Pak's growth

company in the world. In 2013, it made 180 billion of its Briks. Between 1951 and 2014, Tetra Pak increased its market value more than 2800 times, a compound annual growth rate of over 13 percent (see Figure 19).

The Boston Consulting Group (BCG)

In Chapter 5, we told the story of BCG and how it radically simplified top-level consulting. The company and its founder Bruce Henderson have probably been the most important influences on business thinking and practice across the globe since BCG's launch in 1963.

The invention of "strategy consulting" — which combined two previously separate domains of thought (marketing and finance) — has generated remarkable commercial success for the firm itself. Furthermore, BCG has probably had an even greater impact through its alumni, who have become entrepreneurs and venture capitalists, making large personal fortunes for themselves and enriching the world in general. Yet a more narrow, traditional assessment of BCG's success is equally impressive. OC&C (itself a firm of strategy consultants) estimates that the market for top-level strategy consulting grew by 16 percent annually between 1963 and 2014,[10] by which time it stood at more than $21 billion, from a base of only $11 million in 1963 — a 2008-fold increase. Moreover, all of this was achieved with minimal capital. If a similar growth rate were to be maintained for another fifty years, strategy consultants would rule the world. But let's not contemplate such an appalling prospect!

Instead, we should note OC&C's current (theoretical)

valuation of BCG — $15.8 billion. Using the same methodology, the previous market leader — McKinsey — would now be worth $32.1 billion. However, because it was a much larger company in 1963, McKinsey has grown by "only" 761 times (ultimately based on its revenues), whereas BCG has grown by more than 28,500 times! BCG's value outperformance figure against its chief rival is therefore approximately 37 — a reasonable dividend for being the biggest simplifier in the industry it founded.

Note the word "theoretical" in the above calculations. Monetizing the theoretical value of professional services firms such as McKinsey and BCG is notoriously difficult. The successful IPO of Goldman Sachs, however, has shown that it can be done. Admittedly, Goldman Sachs is an investment bank, not a strategy house, and it has the advantage of deploying huge amounts of capital and technology. Yet it ultimately depends on its human capital, just as the strategy consultants do. The most significant difference between the two sectors lies in investment bank employees' desire and determination to get rich quick, compared to a more relaxed attitude on that score among consultants.

The truth is that strategy consultants, in general, have little desire to monetize themselves. It is not in their culture. Marvin Bower strove throughout his long career as the leader and then the godfather of McKinsey to make "the Firm" — always with a capital "F" — a *professional* firm, which for him really did mean putting the clients' interests ahead of those of the Firm. That ethos is almost as strong in BCG, because Bruce Henderson was also more interested in influence and ideas than money. As a result, McKinsey and BCG, and most other strategy houses, are effectively cooperatives that are owned and controlled by their staff. Neither cooperatives nor their leaders become billionaires.

So BCG is probably not "worth" $15.8 billion, because it will never go public. That is a self-imposed limitation (and, incidentally, one that I have never understood), yet it does nothing to detract from the firm's achievements; and the comparison with McKinsey is entirely fair. So the value estimate may be unrealistic, but the relative performance is unarguable, and it is all based on brilliant simplifying.

In the next chapter we summarize company performance in all twelve simplifying case studies and look at other aspects of the comparative performance of simplifiers and non-simplifiers.

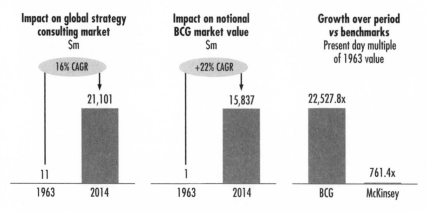

Figure 20: BCG's growth

The Success of Simplifying

An Archaeological Dig

Most of us spend too much time on the last twenty-four hours and too little on the last six thousand years.

Will Durant

In this penultimate chapter, we dig deep to uncover the economic forces that cut across the two simplifying alternatives. We also summarize the results of the twelve case studies, and look at OC&C's further research, which compares industries that innovate through simplicity with those that innovate by other means.

How Do the Companies Fare in Terms of Increasing Their Market Value?

Figure 21 shows each of our twelve companies' growth in market value from the start to the end of their respective

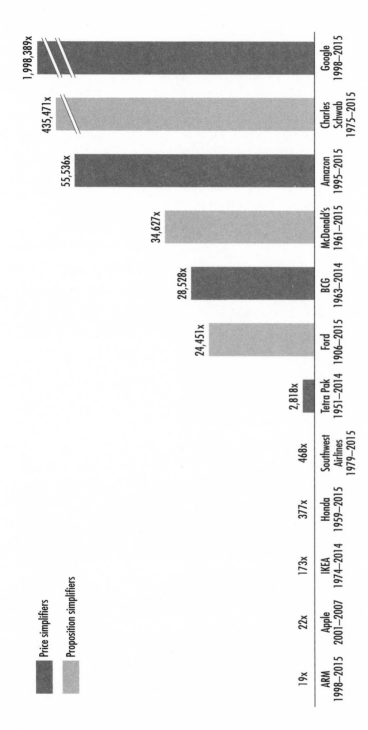

Figure 21: Market value growth

study periods. First, though, a caveat is necessary. These time periods vary enormously, ranging from just six years for Apple's iPod era — when the company's growth was almost dependent on the success of that device — to 109 years for Ford. So, as you look at the figure, take the time periods into account — they are given at the bottom — and apply a mental corrective. (We will eliminate the effect of the differences in time periods in Figures 22 and 23.)

But why should we look at how much each company's value multiplied at all? The answer is that, as you will see, there is very high variation among the cases. All of the growth levels are high when compared with more conservative firms, but they range from a "mere" 19-times increase for ARM to an almost 2,000,000-times increase for Google. Given this degree of variation, the number of years in the different cases is of secondary importance.

Three points stand out from Figure 21:

- The increases are astonishingly high in six cases — ranging from more than 20,000 times to almost 2,000,000 times.
- All twelve simplifiers have enjoyed high growth, and there is no evidence that price-simplifying is better than proposition-simplifying, or vice versa. While twelve cases is a very small sample, we may surmise that, for the highest returns, it does not matter which type of simplifying is employed. Certainly, either approach can lead to stunning increases.
- If we ask why Ford, BCG, McDonald's, Amazon, Charles Schwab, and Google have been so outstanding

at multiplying their values, it helps to look at their individual stories and then see whether there are any common patterns — in addition, of course, to their enthusiasm for simplifying.

Ford, Value Multiplied by 24,451 Times

Henry Ford's price-simplifying sparked massive market growth, sustained over more than a century. The company benefited from redefining its industry, designing a new product that established the brand in the critical early years, and from internationalization, especially in Europe.

BCG, Value Multiplied by 28,528 Times

BCG could scarcely be more different from Ford: it is in a service rather than a manufacturing industry; it is a proposition- not a price-simplifier; it is positioned at the top and not in the low-to-middle end of its market; it is driven by intellectual capital rather than investment in factories and inventory. And yet, BCG's and Ford's respective successes can be explained in remarkably similar ways.

BCG redefined the industry of boardroom consulting by inventing a new dominant product which founder Bruce Henderson labelled "strategy consulting." For half a century the strategy consulting market grew at 16 percent each year; and BCG's revenue growth was even higher at 22 percent per annum.[1] Both the market and BCG's own growth were sustained through international expansion. As we have seen, Ford also reinvented an industry that then grew rapidly around the world for more than fifty years.

In addition, BCG benefited from two factors that are typical of proposition-simplifiers:

- First, its margins, which were already high, increased slightly over time. This enabled the firm to recruit the very best raw intellectual firepower . . . and in turn that firepower justified and sustained the high margins.
- Second, unlike Ford, BCG could expand rapidly without the need to raise much capital. What working capital it had came from deferred payments to staff, which enabled BCG to avoid dependence on external capital.

McDonald's, Value Multiplied by 34,627 Times

Once again, the explanation here broadly follows the Ford/BCG pattern: McDonald's created its own market — the "fast-hamburger meal" market — which expanded exponentially over the next sixty years.

The company enjoyed it highest rate of growth — increasing by over 30,000 times at a rate of over 20 percent a year — between 1961 and 2015, the era of Ray Kroc and the system he created. As we have seen, Kroc took the McDonald brothers' brilliantly simple, pared-down and parsimonious system and *mass produced* it through an enormous, unprecedented expansion of outlets. He was able to scale up McDonald's so effectively and quickly because the heart of the system was so simple. It could be multiplied profitably because its economics were so good. The company had substantial capital requirements, but most of them were outsourced initially to insurance companies and then to other capital providers and franchisees.

No doubt the brand and its visual incarnations — the Golden Arches and the Big Mac — were also vital, but the parallels with Ford and BCG are inescapable. Again, international expansion perpetuated a firm's growth over several decades.

Amazon, Value Multiplied by 55,536 Times

Amazon's increased value cannot be explained simply by the parallel growth in a single focused market. The company's growth has been quite sharp and sudden, whereas the online book market has grown by "only" 21 percent each year since the late 1990s. Furthermore, Amazon's share of that market has fallen from 100 percent to between 60 and 65 percent in the same period.

So we have to find another explanation for Amazon's phenomenal success. The answer lies in the company's efficient use of its customer base to expand into other products, deploying its rock-bottom prices and legendary service to make life easier for its customers. Amazon has bulldozed its way into almost every retail category ... and international expansion has done the rest. But the latter appears to have much further to go.

Charles Schwab, Value Multiplied by 435,471 Times

Charles Schwab follows the Ford/BCG/McDonald's pattern: the firm created huge market growth through its product's simplicity and extreme scalability. Schwab's prices and costs were far lower than those of its competitors, and the company already had all the first-mover advantages when those rivals began to imitate its system — a brand that was synonymous with the product coupled with greater experience and scale which made it impossible for any rival to offer the same deal and still make money. Schwab also benefited from international expansion, although not to the same degree as the other companies at the top of our increased-value list.

Google, Value Multiplied by 1,998,389 Times

Google has diversified prodigiously, but its fortune is still based on the world's simplest and best search engine. Again, it has followed (and extended) the pattern followed by Ford, BCG, McDonald's, and Charles Schwab: Google vastly expanded its market by creating and perfecting the simplest, fastest and most useful search engine; it benefited from the network effects that drew users and advertisers to its site; and it eventually ruled the world.

Of course, there are profound differences, which we have stressed throughout this book, between price-simplifying and proposition-simplifying. What you do and how you do it, and whether you move upmarket or downmarket, largely depend on the type of simplifying you adopt. But it is something of a revelation to learn that the *very* successful simplifiers' value-multiplication formulas cut across both types of simplifying.

Looking at the "archaeological structure of economic success" within our twelve case studies, we can discern two main patterns:

- The route followed by Ford, BCG, McDonald's, Charles Schwab, and Google, as well as by ARM, Southwest Airlines, IKEA, and Tetra Pak. This is based on developing a new, simpler product that is so much cheaper — or so much better to use — than its predecessors that it inflates the market to such an extent that this becomes the platform for an exponential increase in company value. Essential to this mind-blowing growth is a process of internationalization, based on a universal (or nearly universal) product with huge scale and/or network advantages.

- Then there is the route followed by Amazon, Apple, and Honda. Here, the company designs something — an engine, an electronic device, a new way of doing business based on simplifying the customer's experience — that can be replicated in several different markets, one after the other. Each new market or product builds on and reinforces the simplicity and competitive advantage that has already been secured with other products and/or in other markets in a number of ways: For example, by increasing the customer base and selling more items to each customer, which lowers the cost of acquiring more sales; by using the company's skills in a different context, which again lowers costs and reinforces the skill base; by increasing the company's leverage with suppliers and other market participants; and, perhaps most importantly, by growing fast in a new market without the investment and launch costs that a new entrant which lacked skills honed in other markets would face.

How Do the Companies Fare in Terms of *Annual* Increase in Value?

Although the above exploration of absolute increase in market value is interesting, we can make fairer inter-company comparisons by investigating the twelve case studies' compound annual growth rates. Bear in mind, however, that the effect of inflation has not been removed from the figures. Between 1900 and 1950, annual inflation in the United States averaged 2.2 percent; over the next fifty years it was 4 percent; and from 2000 to 2013 it dropped again — to 2.3 percent.[2] So, broadly, it could be argued that we should subtract 2–4 percent from the figures. On the other hand, the OC&C figures do not include dividends — typically 2–4 percent of market value — paid out by each of these companies each year. Consequently, the inflation and dividend effects roughly cancel each other out. Hence, the figures we present here are pretty close to the "real" rates of return.

Any company that makes a real return of 10 percent every year is putting in a very strong performance if it manages to sustain it over a long period of time. A return of 15 percent compounded each year is outstanding. Anything over 20 percent is exceptional; and if this is sustained for a couple of decades, it is the stuff of dreams.

All of the results are impressive. Even so, there is a massive difference between the top performers and the bottom ones. The figures for Google, Amazon, and Apple are obviously astounding. But Tetra Pak, McDonald's, BCG, and Charles Schwab (in ascending order) are particularly noteworthy for maintaining consistently high levels of growth over long periods of time.

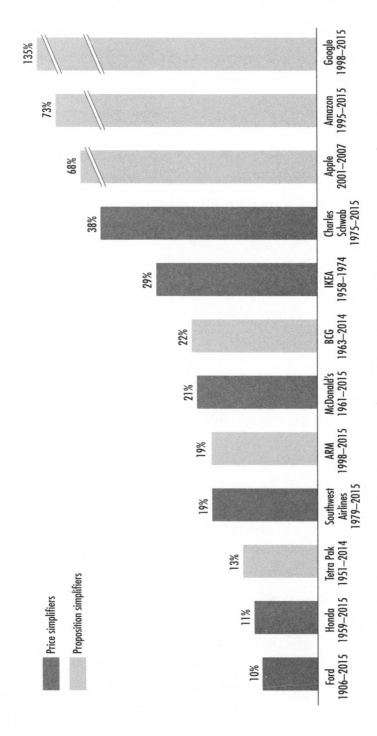

Figure 22: Compound annual increases in market value

How Do the Companies Fare in Terms of Outperformance of Their Rivals?

Our final — and perhaps the best — way to rank our twelve companies is to look at their outperformance of their nearest market rival (or, if there is no comparable rival company, the most relevant stock market index). We decided to exclude Tetra Pak and IKEA from these comparisons because they have no direct competitors for which data are available, and index comparisons would be similarly tricky. (They both originated in Sweden but then became international, and they are both private companies.) So we have compared ten of our companies with their best-performing rivals (or the stock market), and have measured their outperformance of those rivals — defined as a company's increase in market value divided by its main rival's (or the stock market's) increase in value over a certain period of time. This inherently removes the effect of inflation (since it will affect each party equally), and, although it is still imperfect, it is the purest possible measure of comparable performance.

Again, each of the ten companies scores very well — performing at least eleven times better than its nearest rival or index. BCG's and Ford's performances (37 times better and 49 times better than their principal rivals, respectively) are both striking. McDonald's, Charles Schwab's, and Amazon's are out of this world. And a suitable adjective for Google's performance eludes us! Half a million times more growth than its nearest rival is as close to an infinite difference as you will ever see in business. Only a (highly unlikely) repetition of Google's combination of pure simplicity and global network effects will ever deliver anything remotely similar in the future.

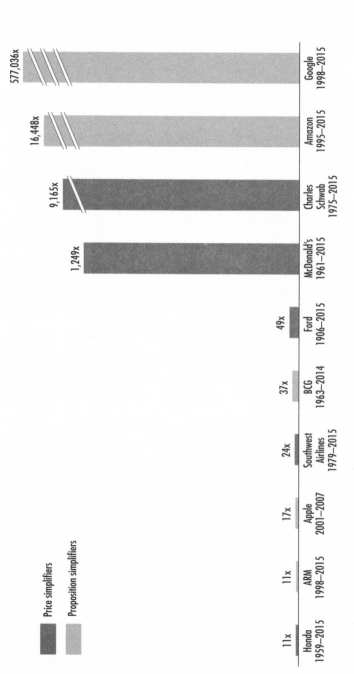

Figure 23: Outperformance (increase in company's market value divided by increase in value of best rival or index over the same period)

Industry-Wide Simplifying

OC&C conducted one final piece of analysis to measure the superiority — or otherwise — of simplifying as a strategy, this time by assessing whole *industries* rather than individual companies. Specifically, they looked into the biotechnology, defense, oil and gas, pharmaceuticals, and soft-drinks industries — all of which have displayed significant innovation over recent years, but not *simplifying* innovation:

- Biotechnology has displayed some tremendous experimentation, but by its nature this is invariably very complex. It does not seem to be a field that lends itself to simplifying.
- The oil and gas industry has grown, but through increasingly complex extraction methods, such as deep-sea exploration and tar sands. Again, there is little evidence of simplifying.
- The pharmaceuticals industry has opted for ever more complex chemical analysis, leading to more complex and increasingly specialized drugs. Research-and-development costs have risen inexorably, and mergers have seemed to discourage or preclude simple innovation by new ventures, as have ever-higher regulatory barriers and costs.
- The defense industry, led by a number of U.S. contractors, has created ever more intricate and powerful weapons while continuing to argue that high capital outlay is necessary to save the lives of service personnel.
- John Stith Pemberton, a tinkering pharmacist, concocted the recipe for Coca-Cola over the course of a

few months in 1886. The company has been unusual ever since as it still derives a large majority of its profits from just three very simple products — Coke itself, Diet Coke and Fanta — although it has tried and failed to diversify into many other drinks over the years. It has been left to smaller companies to bring innovative products to the market, which some of them have done very successfully. However, these new products are increasingly elaborate and segmented, such as diet, vitamin, sports, and many other types of drinks. Hence, the industry and its competitive structure are far more complex than they used to be.

OC&C looked at U.S. stock market growth for these five industries (excluding dividends) from 1994 to 2014, and compared these increases with the growth in five "simplifying" industries: consumer electronics, media, internet, retail, and software. OC&C's analysts chose the latter five industries because of their shared trend towards greater product and service simplicity — lower prices (in some cases dramatically so), greater convenience and ease of use, and smaller yet more powerful devices. Remember, OC&C made no judgement about the simplicity levels of these industries relative to the others; rather, they merely identified five industries that have become more complex and five others that have become simpler over time.

As can be seen from Figure 24, the non-simplifying industries increased in value by between 4 and 15 times, whereas the simplifying industries increased in value by between 5 and 152 times. The mean increases were 6.8 times for the non-simplifying industries and 38.6 times for the

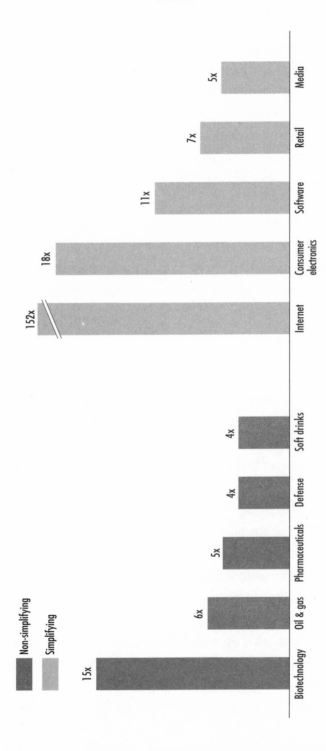

Figure 24: Stock price growth of simplifying and non-simplifying industries, 1994–2014

simplifying industries (although the latter figure was heavily influenced by the huge increase in the internet). The median increases were 5 times for the non-simplifying industries and 11 times for the simplifying industries.

Conclusions

- The twelve case studies of simplifying companies all display very high increases in market value, high annual rates of increase and significant outperformance when compared with rival companies or stock market indices.
- The returns from *both* price-simplifying and proposition-simplifying are very high, with no indication that one type ultimately results in higher financial returns than the other. (The sample sizes are very small, however, so more extensive research might reveal some differences that we have not detected.)
- The increases in value for all twelve of these simplifiers have persisted for decades, even once the major period of simplifying innovation has ended. Eventually, of course, the rewards start to revert to the mean, but they do continue at a high level for a surprising length of time.
- We have emphasized several of the underlying economic reasons for these long-term high returns throughout this book: the increase in market size that results from *either* a 50 percent-plus price cut *or* making a product or service that is a joy to use; the brand and reputational advantages that accrue to a company that succeeds with a radical simplifying innovation; and the lower costs that come from high scale, experience, and/or network

effects. All of these factors combine to make the simplifying company's economics far superior to those of rival firms that fail to simplify to the same extent or even at all. Then all that remains is for the simplifying firm to decide whether to claim its superior returns in further expansion of market share or higher margins. In either case, a virtuous circle is established which continually improves the firm's competitive position and security. It seems that this virtuous circle can persist for a very long time, even without further innovation. These are, however, intuitive and somewhat theoretical explanations. They suggest that price-simplifiers' advantages are somewhat different from those of proposition-simplifiers. The benefit of in-depth case studies that look at returns over long periods, however, is that we can arrive at a deeper and more empirical "archaeological" explanation of how each simplifying company reaps such high and lasting returns. Here we put aside our preconceptions and simply observe how these returns have been generated. We find two distinct patterns: the market explosion pattern and the transformation of customer experience pattern.

The Market Explosion Pattern

In this pattern, the simplifying company creates such a superior new product or service — superior in *either* its remarkably low price *or* in the fact that it is a joy to use — that the product itself multiplies exponentially. The simple new product or service expands the market hundreds or even thousands of times, first through expansion in the

---

domestic market (e.g., North America, Japan, or Europe), then through a relentless process of internationalization. It seems that only simple "universal" products are able to do this. Scale, experience and/or network advantages multiply enormously and tilt the playing field even more towards the simplifying innovator. Both price- and proposition-simplifiers have reaped rich rewards from this process. They include price-simplifiers such as Ford, McDonald's, IKEA, Charles Schwab, and Southwest Airlines, and proposition-simplifiers such as BCG, Tetra Pak, ARM, and Google. (The only partial exception or qualification to the "archaeology" of success outlined in this paragraph is Southwest Airlines, which failed to replicate its formula outside of the United States, leaving it to European budget airlines, notably Ryanair and EasyJet, to internationalize Southwest's innovation.)

The Transformation of Customer Experience Pattern

This transformation works so well in one product or service area that it is then rolled out into other products or services, generating extraordinary growth by invading new competitive territory in a fashion that Genghis Khan, Julius Caesar, or Napoleon would have loved. Honda, Amazon, and Apple have all adopted this approach. This list includes one clear price-simplifier (Honda), one clear proposition-simplifier (Apple) and one company that is certainly a proposition-simplifier but probably also a price-simplifier (Amazon). So we are left in little doubt that the transformation–invasion pattern can work for both types of simplifier.[3]

- In order to maximize the financial returns from their simplifying, it would therefore seem to be advisable for companies to pursue *either* the market explosion pattern *or* the transformation–invasion pattern. However, it might be possible to pursue both simultaneously. Perhaps McDonald's should have ridden not only the "fast-hamburger" market but also the "fast-chicken" and other fast-food markets based on the skills that Ray Kroc perfected: a single-minded focus on very few menu items; very low prices for them; an emphasis on product quality and speedy service; spotless premises and rest rooms; attractions for kids; rigid control of franchisees to ensure consistent quality and economy; site development and financing packages; domination of the U.S. market and then pre-emptive internationalization; and relentless brand-building and promotion over half a century. Kroc rode the market explosion formula almost flawlessly, but he totally missed — or ignored — the opportunity to use his finely honed skills and resources to transform–invade other fast-food markets (with different brands, of course, and probably via different corporations). Perhaps it would have been managerially impossible to do both simultaneously, but Kroc certainly had the template to create fast-food markets in a huge range of product categories.
- Finally, whichever type of simplifying your company pursues, and whichever value maximization pattern you follow, rapid expansion in the domestic market and then around the world is vital. Filling the global market with your simple product or service before your rivals do means the high returns of simplifying have the potential to become astronomical.

18

The Limitations, Power, and Glory of Simplifying

The essence of strategy is that you must set limits on what you're trying to accomplish.[1]

Michael Porter

The difference between stupidity and genius is that genius has its limits.

Albert Einstein

Recall Jan Vermeer's masterpiece, *The Girl with the Pearl Earring* — the torso and head of a young girl against a dark background, turned as if the viewer has suddenly caught her attention, gazing with wide eyes and parted red lips. Her luminous face floats almost three-dimensionally against strong unitary negative spaces. Vermeer knew how to paint not only the girl herself but the background in order to accentuate her beguiling presence.

Everything is like this — defined by the boundary between what a thing is and what it is not — irrespective of whether the thing in question is a tangible object or an ethereal idea. But while you can perceive the limits of an object with your senses, you cannot do the same with the abstract notion that the two types of simplifying represent *the* predominant strategies in business. So it demands significantly more effort to figure out what simplifying is and what it is not.

Are There Any Viable Non-Simplifying Strategies?

Of course there are. Consider the furniture industry, which boasts tens of thousands of firms but only one IKEA. The latter's competitors are not — and cannot all be — successful price- or proposition- simplifiers. Yet there are hordes of them, including a smattering that are rather successful, striving away in the face of IKEA's price-simplifying juggernaut. In one way, the furniture industry is like a natural ecosystem — perhaps a jungle. There are only a few creatures at the top of the food chain, but there are thousands of lesser species with almost infinite variation in physical and reproductive characteristics, defense mechanisms and habitats, as well as myriad passive, predatory, symbiotic and parasitic behaviors, which are in essence naturally selected strategies. These may not be the most powerful strategies, but they have been viable, because the firms are still going. Many other species are now extinct, because *their* strategies have been eclipsed by more successful ones in this evolving marketplace. If we focus solely on the simplifying firms, we are allowing no space on the canvas for the strong, unitary, empty spaces that provide such a contrast to the beautiful creature we are describing. We will be unable to see clearly what is, because we will be unable to see clearly what is not.

Back in the forest of industrial production and commerce, what does that competitive variation look like? What are some of the alternative — and at least temporarily sustainable — competitive strategies? There are three principal ones: *elaborating, invention* and *discovery* strategies.

Elaborating Strategies

Elaborating is the opposite of simplifying: it involves making a product or service more complex. This can be a very successful strategy. Take, for example, *luxury* goods and services. The Patek Philippe Grand Complications wristwatch (in its various forms) retails for tens of thousands of pounds; it is made by hand in very small quantities; and it is terrifically complex mechanically. These are rare and beautiful timepieces, and they function in a world that is antithetical to the "democratic" strategies of price- or proposition-simplifying. With simplified products, even those targeted at customers who are willing to pay a price premium (proposition-simplifying), a larger market is always desirable, and the dream is to develop a universal product that can be mass manufactured. True luxury markets, by contrast, are always niche and deliberately exclusive; the product's complexity and rarity are desirable attributes. The intent is to anoint the privileged few with exclusive opulence and status through fantastic product elaboration — simple functionality and affordability be damned.

Of a similar ilk are *bespoke* products and services: for example, enterprise software — large systems that are tailored to and integrated with a firm's existing systems and practices. Enterprise software is typically replete with important-sounding acronyms: ERP (enterprise resource planning), MIS (management information systems), MRP (materials resource planning), and many others. The requirement to tie together a diverse set of information from numerous sources, with each of those sources either subtly or markedly different with each new deployment, results in incredibly complex products that have to be intimately tailored for each installation. This makes the cost eye-wateringly high, yet the customer often becomes locked in to the system because they feel it is integral to their organization, and switching will cost even more. It's like an addict's relationship with a powerful drug, and the company that supplies the enterprise software reaps rewards of a magnitude that would make a pusher jealous.

The final type of elaborating strategy involves the development of *bigger-is-better* products. These are generally not as commercially successful as luxury or bespoke products over the long term, but they can enjoy quite high growth for a short period. Products might be made bigger — or stronger or faster — in search of scale economy or some specific utility, but in doing so they may become extremely complex, harder to make, and often harder to use. They do, however, represent a meaningful segment of the product universe, where greater complexity is accepted as long as a product performs better than its predecessors — or achieves something that was previously impossible or unavailable. Even though their complexity has high costs — both economic and otherwise — such products still have important roles to play. Consider the behemoth Airbus A380 — a technical marvel that has stretched the physical size of a plane and its engines to the limit of what is feasible, for which its designers deserve great credit. Yet the A380 has also taken Airbus and its customers to the very edge of commercial and operational viability. Among other things, the plane's complexity may prevent it from ever finding a large enough market or commanding a premium margin. Therefore, it may be the latest in a long list of bigger-is-better products — including the Apollo program, the Hummer and Concorde — that eventually disappear.

Invention Strategies

Some inventions simplify; others complicate; and yet others do both. The wheel simplifies. The Airbus A380 complicates. But a coach-and-horses, compared with the horse-and-trap, has *both* simplifying and complicating aspects. Similarly, the car — while demonstrably faster and more comfortable than a horse-drawn coach (proposition-simplifying by being a joy to use) — is obviously a much more complex piece of kit that requires expensive manufacture, skill in both driving and maintenance, and a new, complex infrastructure of roads and traffic controls, in stark contrast to the beautiful simplicity of the equine world.

Is an online meeting or relationship generally superior to a good old-fashioned person-to-person date?

Some inventions are both seductive and commercially successful, up to a point, yet eventually complicate or even compromise our lives and their value. We would be hard pressed to argue, however, that simplifying is a one-way street and always the road more traveled.

Discovery Strategies

Discovering — *finding* something, as opposed to inventing it — can be a very lucrative strategy, even when it does not simplify. The beauty of Seville's gold-encrusted churches and houses rests upon the discovery of America, and the port city's subsequent monopoly on voyages to and from the continent. Again, however, although the discovery of America was hugely lucrative — and in our opinion (not everyone would agree) beneficial — it did not *simplify* the world.

Similarly, think of John D. Rockefeller's mega-successful strategy: "Get up early, strike oil." You can characterize most of the world's mineral-extraction industries in this way — it is a specific strategy that is a far cry from simplifying. Biotechnology is another case in point.

Ways to Escape Market Forces

The three flourishing yet non-simplifying strategies mentioned above do not exhaust the list. There is another set of dimensions, which we may broadly categorize as successful strategies to escape the market forces of perfect competition. These strategies can simplify, but they are much more likely to add complexity.

Market forces are a great leveler — they push you towards becoming a commodity producer and they destroy your profits. So good strategy suspends market forces. It creates breathing space and competitive advantage, and it preserves market share and profits. There are myriad tactics and non-market phenomena which, if combined with the strategic pathways we've discussed, can create the enormous competitive variation that makes markets resemble natural ecosystems. Several of them are listed below.

- Network effects: This is when product or service characteristics improve as the number of customers or participants rises. Imagine a closed (non-interoperable) instant-messaging network. It would be next to useless if only a few people were connected, but tremendously useful if everyone were to connect. The service improves as the number of users increases, and it becomes increasingly difficult for a smaller competitor to offer a viable alternative. Network effects can be so strong that even a substantially better-designed product will fail to make headway against a powerful market leader, because the number of users is so crucial. Businesses like this tend to destroy their competitors; market structure tends towards monopoly or oligopoly. This is suspension of market forces writ large. Sometimes — think Google, Amazon, or Facebook — networks are based on simplifying. But at other times — think telecom networks, banking networks, hub-and-spoke networks (such as airline destinations), or multinational institutions (such as the European Union) — the network combines a little simplifying with a great deal of added complexity.
- Regulation: There is nothing like having a government or other authority tell your would-be competitors that they must cease operation, or force them to jump

through so many hoops that market entry becomes a daunting, risky and/or prohibitively expensive enterprise. This is another way in which market forces are suspended, and many firms specialize in operating within highly regulated markets, reaping rich rewards as a result.

- Intellectual property: This is another form of regulation, although a somewhat more meritocratic one. In the best instances, protecting intellectual property provides an incentive to embark on the lonely and uncertain path to invention. In the worst, though, it allows unscrupulous patent trolls to extort money by exploiting a flawed legal system.

- Lock-in and switching costs: It is not unusual for companies with an inferior product but a large installed base of users to make strong profits year after year. Possessing the best product can seem almost irrelevant in these circumstances, at least for a period of time.

- Personal relationships: We are social creatures who crave the comfort of relationships with other human beings. That is admirable, but it leaves some of us vulnerable to the blandishments of the honey-tongued fraudster. There is nothing like a strong personal relationship to cloud judgement and suspend a market force.

- Scarcity: Some things are naturally scarce. By definition, they cannot be replicated, so they cannot be directly attacked. Just ask the owner of Villa D'Este on Lake Como whether he would be happy to swap it for another hotel. Similarly, the owner of cats.com would be unlikely to let that particular URL go for a song.

- Niche effects: Sometimes a market is so small and specialized that, once occupied, no competitor will be interested in launching an attack. At a certain point market efficiency just doesn't seem to work — the costs of entry can be too high if the market is unable to support two players, which allows the incumbent to enjoy profitable solitude.
- Government: Organizations both great and small are protected from market forces by government intervention. Sometimes half of a nation's total economy might be insulated from competition in this way. Governments rarely simplify; indeed, they nearly always complicate.
- Not-for-profit organizations: The junior cousin of government, often sponsored, appropriately enough, by moguls (both living and dead) who made their fortunes by evading market forces.

Given the extent of this list, it is amazing that the economy works *at all* to increase the wealth of nations and individuals over time. As we can see, a substantial majority of all economic activity either largely or totally escapes market forces. This is the greatest manifestation and vindication of the 80/20 principle.

Simplifying in the Big Picture

Simplifying, then, is not the only viable strategy; nor is it the only way to make a fortune. There are numerous non-simplifying strategies that work perfectly for their practitioners. Nevertheless, two cardinal points should be remembered.

The first is that the large majority of business returns accrue to simplifiers. Admittedly, we have not proved this rigorously; indeed, researching it further would make a very good doctoral study. But given the returns enjoyed by the simplifiers discussed in this book — returns that far exceed the average, sometimes over many decades — we are confident that simplifying sits at the apex of the business food chain. Simplifying companies are almost certainly a small minority of the total universe of firms, yet they generate the majority of total economic value. For anyone interested in high returns, simplifying is a dominant strategy — probably *the* dominant strategy. If you are a business person, you must investigate whether your firm can find a path to simplify and so vastly increase its value. If you conclude that it cannot, you might consider starting a new business to simplify with a blank slate. As a business person, you also need to know whether your company is currently — or may become — dangerously exposed to a price- or proposition-simplifying competitor. If it is, you had better figure out how to evade or defeat your prospective rival ... or sell the business before the threat materializes.

If the first cardinal point is economic and financial, the second is broader. From a consumer and human perspective, the significance of simplifying strategies is intriguing. One of the most fundamental, defining aspects of humanity, even since we began to fashion tools from flint, is the way we have continued to be bound up with technology in the broadest sense of the term. We have created our own environment through technology, one that is nestled within yet transcends nature.

This techno-human environment, although highly

enriching in many ways, immensely stimulating and able to relieve suffering, is also inescapable and unrelenting in its evolutionary pace. It is the simplifying strategies that are able to deliver the benefits of technology — via highly useful and/or affordable products and services — in ways that are relatively human-friendly. Without them, and the relief they bring, we would be in danger of drowning in the torrential waves of technological progress, and might forget that the main justification for business is not the money it makes for some but the good it does for many.

Almost all of the non-simplifying ways of evading market forces mentioned earlier in this chapter are good for the businesses that pursue them and therefore for their employees and owners. But they are not so good for the rest of us; indeed, sometimes they actively work against our interests.

The joy and justification of simplifying is that entrepreneurs and their teams can evade market forces and make fortunes, but also know that what they are doing is good for the rest of society too.

How will the fifty-dollar smartphone change the lives of African villagers? How will artificial intelligence change all of our lives and especially those of our children? How will quantum computing or the next big leap forward in the internet deliver advances that we never thought possible?

No matter how the future plays out, you can bet that it will be simplifiers who deliver benevolent change in acceptable, affordable, and exciting ways.

So where does this leave you at the end of our excursion?

We hope you cannot wait to simplify. But don't expect your new path to be easy:

- Simplifying is not a magic bullet, nor an infallible formula for success.
- You must come up with a radical simplifying idea.
- Then you must develop a product or service that is dramatically simpler than any existing product or service — something that is much simpler to make (and therefore at least 50 percent cheaper) or so much simpler to use that your customers will pay a premium to do so.
- Moreover, the product or service must be so simple that it has the potential to become universal. Geography, culture and other barriers to universal use must be conquered or transcended, not necessarily immediately, but certainly at some point in the not too distant future. Ray Kroc, for example, probably did not have Azerbaijan in his sights when he took control of McDonald's. But nowadays any delay in making a simple product or service universal is becoming increasingly hazardous.
- The business system must be redesigned too, so that the new product and the company both sit at the center of a new web. Customers, suppliers, and other important players, such as franchisees, must all be part of that system, sitting in concentric circles around the product and the company, like planets around the sun.
- Equally, rivals must be banished to the periphery of the system, or excluded altogether. They may be allowed to retreat to areas where the company and product do not wish to compete, but they must not be allowed to challenge the dominance of the new product in its heartland market.
- The product or service must be internationalized

before imitators can launch their versions.

- Simplifying is a creative affair, but it is also intensely practical. Combining the two is hard.

Yet the gods of economics and customer psychology favor the simplifier. A small and relatively new firm — one that commits to following one of the two simplifying strategies and adapts it to suit its own industry — can hit the jackpot.

Furthermore, simplifiers, in addition to benefiting themselves, will surely help society and everyone in it to a much greater degree than non-simplifiers.

Finally, although there are limits to the genius of simplifying, there is no limit to the number of simple universal products than can be imagined and created.

Go forth and simplify!

The Next Steps for Entrepreneurs

Visit www.simplify.fm for:

- Exclusive video clips of Richard Koch explaining how to simplify.
- The Star Principle Quiz and scorecard.
- Further support and materials for entrepreneurs who wish to simplify.
- A community forum for simplifying entrepreneurs.

The Next Steps for Corporate CEOs

Visit www.SIMPLIFYforCEOs.com for:

- An interactive guide to simplifying for established companies.
- An interactive quiz to help you decide between price- and proposition-simplifying.
- How to spot incipient simplifying among new ventures.
- How to counter simplifying among new ventures.
- A community forum for leading companies wishing to simplify or facing threats from simplifying rivals.

Why Two Websites?

- Simplifying is a two-sided battle between established leading firms and new simplifying ventures.
- Go to where you will find like-minded people who can offer the tips and support you need.

Endnotes

Preface by Richard Koch

1 Richard Koch (2008) *The Star Principle: How It Can Make You Rich*, London: Piatkus.
2 "Sunday Times Rich List 2015', *Sunday Times Magazine*, 26 April 2015, page 72: "Richard Koch £180m'.

The Secret Is Out!

1 Henry Ford (1922) *My Life and Work*, London: William Heinemann, pages 68–9.
2 Ray Kroc (1977) *Grinding It Out: The Making of McDonald's*, Chicago: Contemporary Books, pages 70–1.
3 Walter Isaacson (2011) *Steve Jobs*, New York: Simon & Schuster, page 126.
4 Ibid., page 564.
5 Leander Kahney (2008/2009) *Inside Steve's Brain*, London: Atlantic Books, page 96.

Chapter 1: The Man Who Democratized Travel

1 Ford, op. cit., page 64.
2 Ibid., page 67.
3 Ibid., page 73.
4 Ibid., pages 67–8.
5 Ibid., page 58.

6 Ibid., page 72.
7 Ibid., page 69.
8 Ibid., page 66.
9 Ibid., page 74.
10 Ibid., page 68.
11 See Chapter 15.

Chapter 2: The Billionaire Who Travels by Bus

1 "He Lives in a Bungalow, Flies EasyJet and "Dries Out" Three Times a Year ... The Man who Founded Ikea and is Worth £15bn', *Daily Mail*, 14 April 2008, www.dailymail.co.uk/news/article-559487/ He-lives-bungalow-flies-easyJet-dries-times-year-man-founded-Ikea-worth-pound-15bn.html, retrieved 3 November 2009.
2 Ingvar Kamprad (1976) *The Testament of a Furniture Dealer*, Delft, The Netherlands: Inter IKEA Systems BV.
3 Quoted in Chris Zook and James Allen (2012) Repeatability: Building Enduring Businesses for a *World of Constant Change*, Boston, MA: Harvard Business Review Press, pages 99–100.
4 "He Lives in a Bungalow," op. cit.
5 Kamprad, op. cit.

Chapter 3: The Assembly Line of Food

1 Quoted in Chip Heath and Dan Heath (2008) *Made to Stick: Why Some Ideas Take Hold and Others Come Unstuck*, London: Arrow, page 28.
2 Kroc, op. cit., pages 6–8 (adapted; the quotes are verbatim).
3 "The "Average" McDonald's by the Numbers', *Burger Business*, 8 February 2012, www.burgerbusiness.com/?p=9385, retrieved 3 November 2012.
4 Kroc, op. cit., page 100.
5 Ibid., pages 11–12.
6 Ibid., see photographs on pages 106–7.
7 Ibid., page 71.
8 Ibid., page 113.
9 Ibid., pages 77–8.
10 Ibid., page 113.
11 Ibid., page 115.
12 Ibid., page 100.
13 Ibid., page 159.

Chapter 4: Victory over Big Brother

1 *Business Week*, 3 October 1983.
2 Quoted in Isaacson, op. cit., page 169.
3 Ibid., page 59.
4 Kahney, op. cit., pages 72–6; Isaacson, op. cit., page 73.
5 Isaacson, op. cit., pages 125–6.
6 Ibid., page 97.
7 Ibid., page 99.
8 Ibid., pages 95–100, 491.
9 Ibid., page 110.
10 Ibid., page 195.
11 Ibid., page 356.
12 Ibid., page 562.
13 Ibid.

Chapter 5: The Strategy Simplifiers

1 We do not mean to imply that the leaders of BCG were being hypocritical. I don't think that the discrepancy occurred to them, or that they really thought about their firm as a "business" in the same sense as their clients had businesses. If they had, they might have come to the realization (rather earlier than they did) that there are two kinds of customers and markets, each of which requires a different strategy: one based on price and volume; the other on proposition and margin.

Chapter 6: Taxi! The Brave New World of Apps

1 "Uber looks to flag down a $10 bn valuation." *The Financial Times.* http://www.ft.com/cms/s/0/c4a403a6-dc71-11e3-9016-00144feabdc0.html.
2 "Uber Confirms New $1.25B Funding Round At $40B Valuation." *TechCrunch.* http://techcrunch.com/2014/12/04/uber-confirms-new-1-2b-funding-round-looks-to-asia-for-expansion/.
3 "Uber eyes $50 Billion Valuation in New Funding." *WSJ.com.* www.wsj.com/articles/uber-plans-large-new-funding-round-1431137142.
4 "Uber Refueling Its Warchest Yet Again, At A Valuation Of Up To $70BN." *Techcrunch.* techcrunch.com/2015/10/24/one-more-billion/. Retrieved 24 October 2015.
5 "Uber is Generating A Staggering Amount Of Revenue." *Business Insider.* http://uk.businessinsider.com/uber-revenue-projection-in-2015-2014-11.

6 "Chicago — Uber's biggest launch to date?" Newsroom.
uber.com. http://blog.uber.com/2011/09/22/
chicago-ubers-biggest-launch-to-date/.
7 "I'm a Bob the Builder" — Oliver Samwer at CEO Berlin'.
venturevillage.eu/ceo-berlin-im-a-bob-the-builder-oliver-samwer.
8 "Tech's Fiercest Rivalry: Uber vs. Lyft." *WSJ.com*. www.wsj.com/
articles/two-tech-upstarts-plot-each-others-demise-1407800744.
9 "Exclusive: Google is developing its own Uber competitor."
Bloomberg Business. www.bloomberg.com/news/articles/2015-02-02/
exclusive-google-and-uber-are-going-to-war-over-taxis.
10 "An analysis of the labor market for Uber drivers." *Scribd.com*. www.scribd.
com/doc/253410228/An-Analysis-of-the-Labor-Market-for-Uber-Drivers.

Chapter 7: The Two Strategies and Their Trade-offs

1 Horst Boog, Gerhard Krebs and Detlef Vogel (2006) *Germany and the
Second World War*, Volume VII: *The Strategic Air War in Europe and
the War in the West and East Asia, 1943–1944/5*, Oxford: Clarendon
Press, page 407.
2 http://vintagepenguins.blogspot.co.uk/p/review-of-penguin-books.
html, retrieved 15 August 2014.
3 George Orwell, "Review of Penguin Books," *New English Weekly*,
5 March 1936, http://vintagepenguins.blogspot.co.uk/p/review-of-
penguin-books.html, retrieved 15 August 2014.

Chapter 8: Which Type of Simplifier Will You Be?

1 Karl Marx (1863/1995) *Capital*, edited by David McLellan, Oxford:
Oxford University Press, pages 291–2.
2 See both the report and appendices in Boston Consulting Group
(1975) *Strategy Alternatives for the British Motorcycle Industry*, London:
Her Majesty's Stationery Office.
3 United States Bureau of the Census (1980) *Statistical Abstract of the
United States*, Washington, DC: United States Bureau of the Census,
page 648, quoted in Clayton Christensen (1997) *The Innovator's
Dilemma: When New Technologies Cause Great Firms to Fail*, Boston,
MA: Harvard Business School Press, pages 152, 158.
4 Richard S. Tedlow (1990) *New and Improved: The Story of Mass
Marketing in America*, New York: Basic Books, pages 22–111. The
market share data are on page 88, and the financial data on pages
92–3.

5 Ibid., pages 168–9.
6 Ibid., page 171.
7 Ibid., pages 169–75.
8 See Richard Rumelt (2011) *Good Strategy, Bad Strategy: The Difference and Why It Matters*, New York: Crown Business, page 221.

Chapter 9: How to Proposition-Simplify

1 Quoted in Peter Burrows, "The Seed of Apple's Innovation," *Business Week*, 12 October 2004, page 188.
2 Kahney, op. cit., page 109.
3 http://designmuseum.org/design/jonathan-ive, retrieved 14 June 2014.
4 Kahney, op. cit., page 91.
5 Ibid., page 96.
6 As mentioned above, price-simplifiers normally *reduce* variety to cut costs. But proposition-simplifiers have a different agenda: to make their product or products better. This sometimes entails *increasing* product range.
7 Brad Stone (2007) "Facebook Expands into MySpace's Territory," *New York Times*, 25 May, www.nytimes.com/2007/05/25/technology/25social.html?_r=0, retrieved 16 June 2014.
8 Isaacson, op. cit., page 126.
9 Ibid., page 133.
10 Ibid., page 78.
11 Tedlow, op. cit., page 168.
12 Stone, op. cit.

Chapter 10: How to Price-Simplify Part I

1 "Southwest Airlines: A Brief History," www.southwest.com, quoted in Southwest's Wikipedia entry, retrieved 2 November 2012.
2 Based on 2011 data, "Scheduled Passengers Carried, International Air Transport Association," quoted in Southwest's Wikipedia entry, retrieved 2 November 2012.
3 James Carville and Paul Begala (2002) *Buck up, Suck up, and Come Back when You Foul up*, New York: Simon & Schuster, page 88.
4 Ibid., page 3.
5 Diane Coyle (1997) *The Weightless World: Strategies for Managing the Digital Economy*, Oxford: Capstone, page vii.
6 Henry Ford (1926) *Today and Tomorrow*, London: William Heinemann, page 14.

7 Ibid., page 68.

8 Ibid., page 15.

Chapter 11: How to Price-Simplify Part II

1 Henry Ford, *Today and Tomorrow*, op. cit., page 15.

2 Tedlow, op. cit., page 128.

3 The "Merry Oldsmobile" — really a motorized buggy and not strictly comparable with Ford's family car — was by far the largest-selling car model before the Model T. In 1904 it sold 5000 units, making it the market leader, before disappearing after Ransom E. Olds fell out with his financiers. The Model T sold 5986 in 1908, 12,292 the following year and 577,036 in 1916. Ibid., pages 119–25.

4 Ibid., page 123.

5 Ford, op. cit., page 80.

6 Tedlow, op. cit., page 274.

7 Ibid., page 261.

8 www.aboutschwab.com/about, retrieved 18 January 2015.

9 about.vanguard.com/who-we-are/fast-facts/.

10 http://www.statista.com/statistics/235553/assets-managed-in-mutual-funds-worldwide/.

11 Christensen, op. cit.

12 Ibid., page xv.

13 Ibid., page xx.

14 Ibid., page xxi.

15 Ibid., page xxiii.

16 Ibid., page 93.

Chapter 13: The Weakness of Strong Firms

1 Tom Peters (1992) *Liberation Management: Necessary Disorganization for the Nanosecond Nineties*, New York: Alfred A. Knopf, page 489.

2 Christensen, op. cit., page 106.

3 Rumelt, op. cit., pages 135–7.

4 Theodore Levitt (1960) "Marketing Myopia," *Harvard Business Review*, July–August, pages 45–56.

5 Christensen, op. cit., pages 115–17.

6 Ibid., pages 104–5.

7 Ibid., pages 135–7.

Chapter 14: How Market Leaders Can Simplify Without Tears

1 Christensen, op. cit., page 153.
2 Gordon Moore, Intel's co-founder and chairman, initially described IBM's use of the 8088 microprocessor in its PC as just a "small design win" for his company. See George W. Cogan and Robert A. Burgelman (1994) "Fading Memories: A Process Theory of Strategic Business Exit in Dynamic Environments," *Administrative Science Quarterly*, 39 (1), pages 24–56; quoted in Christensen, op. cit., page 154 and 158.
3 Christensen, op. cit., pages 111–15.
4 Isaacson, op. cit., page 213.
5 http://gizmodo.com/5910223/how-yahoo-killed-flickr-and-lost-the-internet, retrieved 27 April 2015.

Chapter 15: Does Price-Simplifying Pay?

1 OC&C estimates based on data in John F. Love (1995) *McDonald's: Behind the Arches*, New York: Bantam, pages 12 and 152.
2 Authors' calculation based on McDonald's revenues of $2.6 million in 1961 (ibid., page 152) and $27,441 million in 2014 (McDonald's annual report).
3 This compares with a 2012 Bloomberg Billionaires Index estimate of €52.4 billion for Ingvar Kamprad's total wealth. The latter was technically incorrect, as Kamprad does not own the empire personally, but it can be taken as a reasonable estimate of the total value of all IKEA entities.
4 See an intriguing summary of the strategy debate in Richard P. Rumelt (1995) "The Many Faces of Honda," www.anderson.ucla.edu/faculty/dick.rumelt/Docs/Papers/HONDA, retrieved 16 September 2015.
5 Boston Consulting Group, op. cit.

Chapter 16: Does Proposition-Simplifying Pay?

1 Isaacson, op. cit., pages 388–9.
2 "The Fall of Facebook," *The Atlantic*, December 2014, page 35.
3 Rumelt, *Good Strategy, Bad Strategy*, op. cit., page 14.
4 Isaacson, op. cit., pages 386 (Rubenstein) and 384 (Schiller).

5 Ibid., pages 389–90.

6 Ibid., page 393.

7 Timothy Prickett Morgan (2011) "ARM Holdings Eager for PC and Server Expansion," *The Register*, 1 February, www.theregister. co.uk/2011/02/01/arm_holdings_q4_2010_numbers/, retrieved 15 September 2015.

8 Frederick C. Ingram's chapter on Tetra Pak, *The Gale Directory of Company Histories*, www.answers.com/topic/tetra-pak-international-s-a, retrieved 8 December 2014.

9 Peter Andersson and Tommy Larsson (1988) *Historien om dynastin Rausing*, Stockholm: Norstedts, page 23.

10 This may be an understatement, because OC&C has conservatively included McKinsey's 1963 revenues in the market size. A different definition would include only the BCG revenues, since in 1963 it was the only firm in the world to be practicing the new approach on the basis of the emergent methodology. Only in the late 1960s did McKinsey begin to offer anything approaching a similar service. If we were to say that the strategy consulting market in 1963 comprised only BCG's revenues, then the market has increased by 149,000 times since that year — a compound annual growth rate of 26.9 percent.

Chapter 17: The Success of Simplifying

1 Readers may wonder how this can be possible, given that BCG invented the market and went from 100 percent market share to something significantly lower. The answer is that McKinsey's boardroom consulting revenues for 1963 are included in OC&C's definition of the strategy consulting market.

2 The corresponding UK figures were a little higher: 2.3, 6.2 and 3 percent, respectively (www.measuringworth.com for increases in the Consumer Price Index; authors' calculations for compound annual growth rates).

3 Strategists may note that the distinction between these two patterns is somewhat similar to the difference between the BCG/Michael Porter theory of competitive advantage (based on individual market segment advantage) and the Pralahad/ Hamel theory of "core competences' (as well as resource theory

generally). However, our conclusion arose from *empirical examination* of how the extraordinary returns of our twelve simplifiers accrued in practice. We therefore hope that a more "universal," consensus theory of competitive advantage may emerge in due course.

Chapter 18: The Limitations, Power, and Glory of Simplifying

1 http://www.fastcompany.com/42485/michael-porters-big-ideas

Acknowledgments

I (Richard) can't remember exactly who suggested I should write this book, but I think it was some combination of Chris Outram, Greg Lockwood, my publisher Tim Whiting, and my agent Sally Holloway, after I had mentioned the possibility. And if it wasn't them, but something autonomous in my brain, all four of them certainly encouraged me, so they are at least partly to blame. If the book strikes a chord, then I shall thank them profusely. If it doesn't, I shall hold them entirely responsible for wasting my time over the past four years.

In all seriousness, Greg and I owe a big debt of gratitude to Chris, Tim, and Sally. Let me deal with Chris and his organization first.

Chris Outram is the founder and chairman emeritus of OC&C Strategy Consultants, and I remember discussing the idea for the book with him over lunch in a strangely "English" pub somewhere in the Algarve, after finding all the Portuguese restaurants we wanted to visit were closed. Chris instantly liked the idea, and roped in one of his partners, Nic Farhi, who was also keen to get involved. He might not have been so keen if he had known how long the journey would be and how much time and work would be involved! Although Chris and Nic were often quite blunt about the inadequacies of early drafts, they were also unfailingly engaged and never complained. They and many of their OC&C colleagues made a terrific contribution to the ideas contained in these pages and the way they were eventually structured.

OC&C undertook an extensive research program for the book, uncovering and estimating data on some obscure markets with great diligence and ingenuity. This project was ably led by Aveek Bhattacharya, with first-class support from Richard Brooks, Greg Coates, Matt Cummins, Meilene Lam, and Chris Smith.

Tim Whiting, Publisher at Piatkus, has been whole-heartedly behind the book from start to finish, and his team has been consistently professional. It has been a joy to work with them all.

Nobody could wish for a better agent than Sally Holloway — she has been most patient and supportive yet also perceptive and direct when necessary.

Great thanks also to two academic experts in business strategy — Professors Andrew Campbell and David J. Collis — and to the well-known American marketing guru Perry Marshall. Andrew, a founder and director of the Ashridge Strategic Management Center in London, kindly read several drafts of the book and made appropriately penetrating and incisive comments — not least regarding the need to make the text as simple as possible. It was hard not to be discouraged by his comments at times, but — as usual — he was totally right. The book has benefited immeasurably from his input.

A million years ago, David was one of my colleagues at BCG. He is now the Thomas Henry Carroll Ford Foundation Adjunct Professor at Harvard Business School. Like Andrew, David also generously slogged through several drafts of *Simplify* and urged us to address half a dozen critical points, which we did. He was also responsible for highlighting that customers' willingness or unwillingness to pay a premium for a product is an important factor to consider when choosing between proposition- and price-simplifying. His thinking strongly influenced Figure 1: The simplifying opportunity chart in Chapter 7.

Perry is the author of the world's most popular book on internet advertising — *Ultimate Guide to Google Adwords* — as well as *80/20 Sales and Marketing*. In addition to commenting helpfully on many drafts of *Simplify*, his pivotal intervention was to invite me to be the main speaker at a three-day event in Chicago attended by a large number of entrepreneurs and CEOs from around the world. One day of the seminar was devoted to a trot through the *Simplify* theory, and the experience convinced me that we were on to something big. Perry has contributed significantly to the ideas in the book and he has been a constant source of intellectual stimulation and inspiration.

We are also grateful to the many other people who read drafts of the book and suggested improvements. I would particularly like to mention Andrin Bachmann, Natasha Ratanshi, and Aidan Montague, who all went out their way to help.

Josh Douglas, my business manager, made innumerable useful comments on the text and contributed plenty of practical advice. He also drew the figures.

My partner, the songwriter and surprise new pop star Matthew Grimsdale, has been a tower of strength throughout the project, and made me keep at it when I would otherwise have thrown in the towel.

Finally, many thanks to the 150 people who attended the Simplify seminar in Chicago. You were great participants and the material was hugely validated and enhanced by your comments and enthusiasm. Any reader wishing to see highlights of the event can find them on www.simplify.fm.

About the Authors

Richard Koch is the bestselling author of *The 80/20 Principle*, which has sold over a million copies and been published in thirty-three languages. He is also a highly successful entrepreneur and investor whose ventures have included Filofax, Plymouth Gin, Belgo and Betfair. He was formerly a partner of Bain & Company and co-founder of LEK Consulting. He is also the author of more than 20 highly acclaimed non-fiction books. He lives in Gibraltar.

Greg Lockwood is a founder of Piton Capital, a London-based venture capital firm that invests in businesses with network effects. He has a Masters of Management degree from the Kellogg Graduate School of Management, and is the co-author of *Superconnect* with Richard Koch.

Index

Diagrams are indicated in **bold** and tables in *italics*.

vanadium steel 6–7, 9, 148
Vanguard Group 167–168
venture capital 171
Vermeer, Jan 267–268
Vespa scooter 133–134
viral advertising 64, 70, 74

Walkman 127, 130, *131*, 209
Walmart 161
Walton, Sam 196
Wang 178
warning signals tests 180–183
watches 148, 269
Waze 211
website 96, 183, 212, 280, 281
Westinghouse 198–199
WhatsApp 211–212
Wikipedia 178

Wonga 128, 130, *131*
Woolco 205–206
Woolworth's 86, 205–206
word-of-mouth advertising 64, 70, 74
workforce specialization 11
Wozniak, Steve 35
WYSIWYG 36, 117

Xerox 35–36, 40, 81, 115–117, 178, 190–191

Yahoo! 208, 239
YouTube 211

Zen xxii, 240
zero price offerings 134–135
Zipcar 128, 130, *131*